THE GOLDEN ESSENCE IS YOU

THE ARCHANGELS' GUIDE TO THE ASCENSION

MARILYN ZSCHAU BAARS

BALBOA
PRESS
A DIVISION OF HAY HOUSE

Copyright © 2011 Marilyn Zschau Baars, C.C.H.T

Cover Art by Walter Bruneel © 2010 "A Myriad of Golden Angels"-All Rights Reserved
Website: www.walterbruneel.com

All rights reserved. No part of this book may be used or reproduced by any means, graphic, electronic, or mechanical, including photocopying, recording, taping or by any information storage retrieval system without the written permission of the publisher except in the case of brief quotations embodied in critical articles and reviews.

Balboa Press books may be ordered through booksellers or by contacting:

Balboa Press
A Division of Hay House
1663 Liberty Drive
Bloomington, IN 47403
www.balboapress.com
1-(877) 407-4847

Because of the dynamic nature of the Internet, any Web addresses or links contained in this book may have changed since publication and may no longer be valid. The views expressed in this work are solely those of the author and do not necessarily reflect the views of the publisher, and the publisher hereby disclaims any responsibility for them.

The author of this book does not dispense medical advice or prescribe the use of any technique as a form of treatment for physical, emotional, or medical problems without the advice of a physician, either directly or indirectly. The intent of the author is only to offer information of a general nature to help you in your quest for emotional and spiritual well-being. In the event you use any of the information in this book for yourself, which is your constitutional right, the author and the publisher assume no responsibility for your actions.

ISBN: 978-1-4525-0141-3 (sc)
ISBN: 978-1-4525-0143-7 (dj)
ISBN: 978-1-4525-0142-0 (e)

Library of Congress Control Number: 2010917944

Any people depicted in stock imagery provided by Thinkstock are models, and such images are being used for illustrative purposes only.
Certain stock imagery © Thinkstock.

Printed in the United States of America

Balboa Press rev. date: 11/7/2011

DEDICATION

I dedicate this book to my beloved husband and partner in life, Franciscus Joseph Baars.

Frans, you have my eternal love and gratitude for your love, your friendship, your patience, your partnership, and your sage advice, the evidence of which can be seen on every page of this co-creation with the Archangels. You were there for us when the messages were coming in, and you provided the stability and grounding energies that allowed me to hear and repeat the loving information from the Archangels.

Without you, this book would have been infinitely more difficult to bring to fruition. I thank you, with all my heart. *Altijd!*

TABLE OF CONTENTS

DEDICATION	v
ACKNOWLEDGMENTS	xi
INTRODUCTION	xvii
A NOTE TO READERS/LISTENERS	xxvii
FOREWORD FROM THE ARCHANGELS: THE BOOK OF THE ASCENSION	1
Chapter One: The Frequency of Love; Archangel Meditation: The Journey to the Sea of Light and Love	9
Chapter Two: The White, Pink, and Red Roses	19
Chapter Three: Regeneration and Miracles	23
Chapter Four: The Creator's Love and Light; Agreements	31
Chapter Five: Cords of Attachment and How to Release Them	37
Chapter Six: Instructions for Ascension; Simultaneous Time; Energy Infusion	43
Chapter Seven: The Ascension; Raising Your Vibrational Level; About the Affirmations	49

Chapter Eight: The Ascension Vibratory Level; Additional Cord-Cutting Information — 57

Chapter Nine: About Souls and Their Relationships to Humans; Changing Your Contract with Your Soul — 65

Chapter Ten: Change What You Think, Feel, and Believe — 73

Chapter Eleven: Becoming A Channel of Love — 81

Chapter Twelve: The Importance of NOW TIME — 89

Chapter Thirteen: The Aspects of Love; Aliens Among Us — 97

Chapter Fourteen: Lifting the Veil from Your Eyes; The Light Within; Wake Up! — 105

Chapter Fifteen: Thinking With the Heart — 113

Chapter Sixteen: The Field of Golden Essence: A Fifth Dimensional Visualization — 121

Chapter Seventeen: A Visit with the Archangels — 129

Chapter Eighteen: The Being of Light in the Heart; Methods of Managing Emotions — 135

Chapter Nineteen: Visualization: Journey to the Whales and the Dolphins — 143

NOTES ON THE INFORMATION IN CHAPTER TWENTY — 149

Chapter Twenty: NOW TIME; Triad Platforms; Cord-Cutting — 151

Chapter Twenty-One: Triad Platforms — 159

Chapter Twenty-Two: Meeting Your Higher Self	165
Chapter Twenty-Three: Additional Information About Cord-Cutting	173
Chapter Twenty-Four: NOW TIME; Triad Platforms; Miracles	177
Chapter Twenty-Five: More on Cord-Cutting; A Meditation: Journey Through Space	191
Chapter Twenty-Six: Breathe IN The Sun	201
Chapter Twenty-Seven: Agreements Made Before "The Beginning"	207
Chapter Twenty-Eight: Meditation: The Bubble of Golden Light	213
Chapter Twenty-Nine: Absorbing the Incoming Energies	221
Chapter Thirty: The Cleansing Celestial Light Shower	227
Chapter Thirty-One: The Conscious Breathing Project	233
Chapter Thirty-Two: Meditation: In the Beginning...	237
Chapter Thirty-Three: Additional Important Information About Cord-Cutting	245

APPENDICES 251

1. THE AFFIRMATIONS FOR THE JOURNEY TO THE SEA OF LOVE AND LIGHT 253
2. AFFIRMATIONS FROM THIS BOOK 255

3.	THE CORD-CUTTING PROCESS	257
4.	THE CLEANSING CELESTIAL LIGHT SHOWER	261

RESOURCES 263

GLOSSARY 269

ABOUT THE AUTHORS 279

ACKNOWLEDGMENTS

I wish to thank all the people who have helped and supported me from the beginning of my journey on a spiritual path:

To my dear friends Ron and Susan Scolastico: Ron, thanks for those spectacular channeled messages over the years, but especially for that very first one on September 8, 1983 in New York City. And thank you, Susan, for being my friend — how could we miss, with the same birth date?

To my Reiki Master Teacher, Mary Goslen, holder of the Usui-Hayashi-Takata-Fran Brown-Mary Goslen Lineage of Original Reiki: Dearest Mary, you gave me hope in the power of energy and love when my beloved cat Puffy was ill. And he lived on for two more years after his doctors had given up! I'm certain it was that Level One Reiki Initiation he got at your studio that kept him alive so long. Thank you also for teaching me the entire system of Original Reiki; it has been a marvelous tool so often, I've lost count. I'm also certain that the transferral of the Reiki Energy to me began my energetic journey to the Archangels and changed me in ways that I probably am not even aware of today. Lastly, thank you for your friendship over the years. It means the world to me.

For Joan Pancoe, Psychic Therapist: Thanks for those journeys back in "Time"! The experiences opened my eyes even further and helped me change my persona and myself. I still remember that night after my animal regression, when all I could think of was eating venison!! And I found it, in a little French bistro on the West Side. Mmmmm...

To Debbie Kempton-Smith, Astrologer: Thanks, Deb, for the spectacular information and interpretations! I appreciate your sense of humor *so much*. Love your book as well.

To Jay Farnsworth, originator of Subjective Communication: Jay, thanks for everything, especially for the Huna instruction and methods of solving just about any problem!! You're the *best*.

For Eric Pearl, originator of The Reconnection Method of Healing: Eric, I loved your book and I loved your healing course. Thank you for bringing this information in for all of us.

To Richard Gordon, founder of Quantum-Touch: Oh, my, didn't we laugh?? You are a wonderful and inspiring teacher and a great entertainer to boot! You rocked my belief system to the core.

To Alain Herriot: Thank you, Alain, for the Quantum-Touch Advanced Course. You were inspiring.

To Larry Valmore, facilitator and teacher of Psych-K: Thank you, Larry, for the good times in Vilvoorde, Belgium, not only in the classroom, but also in the restaurants. Lots of laughing going on there! And learning, too, of course!

David Quigley, C.C.H.T. and head of The Alchemy Institute of Healing Arts: Thanks, Quiggles, for the regressions especially, and for the wonderful empowerment seminar at Mt. Shasta in 2003, where Archangel Mary came to me with a very important message, just before ALL the Archangels began speaking to me on July 23, 2003. What an experience that was!

For Marilyn Gordon, C.C.H.T., The Center for Hypnotherapy, Oakland, California: My thanks to you, Marilyn, for your lovely presence, filled with love and light, and for your consummate teaching skills. It was a pleasure to study hypnosis with you.

Susan Mokelke, Executive Director of The Foundation for Shamanic Studies: Thank you, Susan, for retrieving all my lost parts. I'll never forget that journey to the Dragon's Lair to retrieve my little girl and how much better I felt for it. You are *brilliant!!*

For Lee Carroll, channel for the Magnetic Master, Kryon: Lee, thank you for your contribution toward the worldwide acceptance of channeling, first of all, but most especially for the amazing and sometimes incredible information Kryon brought to all of us through you. I still cry when I read *The Journey Home* — what a wonderful book with a beautiful, inspiring story. It's magical.

To Steve Rother, channel for The Group: Steve, you have been a *leader* in the field of channeling, and I enjoyed our seminars in Hawai'i so much. Thank you for setting the stage for my partner and friend, my husband, Frans, to meet me in 2004. We both are grateful to you for so many reasons.

For my friend Melainah Yee: Thank you for your guidance and friendship, dearest sister, through all these years since we first met in 2003 (even though we *both* know we are "Family" from the Beginning) in Lemuria. I treasure you more than you can know.

To Henning and Mariana Linde: Thank you both so much for your love and your friendship; Frans and I both give loving thanks to you, our friends in The Netherlands, for facilitating our very first opportunity to channel healing energies from the Archangels at your weekend seminar in Elspeet, in January 2005. Lieve Mariana en Henning: BEDANKT!!

To Kahu Fred Sterling, medium for the angel Kirael, and Patti "Athenna" Sterling: Thank you both for our beautiful wedding, and for your friendship, which we treasure. You are an inspiration, Fred, and Patti, well, you are *my* fairy godmother!! Fred, your Signature Cell Healing is an invaluable method. Thanks for teaching it to me.

For dearest Ronna Herman, channel for the Archangel Michael: Right away, when we first met and you slipped your hand into mine, I *knew* you as my old friend (and I know *you* know what I mean by "old") over many lifetimes. Thank you for everything you are, Ronna, and thank you for my personal messages from Archangel Michael. I love them and I love YOU.

To James Tyberonn, channel for Archangel Metatron: Thank you, Tyb, for taking Frans and me under your wing in March 2009. We grew in confidence under your benevolent guidance, and are grateful to you for the opportunities you provided for us to present The Archangels' wisdom.

To Surja Jessup, C.H.T.: Thank you, Surja, for the meetings with the Archangels you facilitated for me. You are a spectacular alchemical hypnotherapist.

Jim Self, teacher of Mastering Alchemy: Thanks, Jim, for mastering alchemy and teaching it to all of us. Love that Orange Dragonfly!

For my partner in life and beloved husband, Franciscus Joseph Baars: I could not have accomplished this without YOU, my dearest friend in all the universes! I love you AL TIJD.

I wish also to thank all of our Archangel Healing clients for their contributions to my personal comprehension of the healing process and the power of Love. Thank you for giving us your trust and for your cooperation in facilitating your own healings! You are all dear to both of us.

From each of these teachers and friends I have gleaned jewels of knowledge, which make up my necklace of pearls of wisdom. I thank each of them for their contribution to this co-creation the Archangels and I have brought forth.

MOST OF ALL, I GIVE THANKS
TO THE ARCHANGELIC REALM
AND ALL THE ANGELS THEREIN.
WE ARE LOVE AND LIGHT FOREVER
IN THE SOURCE CREATOR
OF ALL THERE IS.

INTRODUCTION

"We are the Archangels and we greet you this day..."

And with these words, my life changed.

On September 8, 1983, I began a quest that led me to study many varied methods of healing over a twenty-year period, culminating with the words written above, which came to me on July 23, 2003, as I sat at my computer. From that day, I have been involved with communicating with the Archangels through messages they give me on a daily basis. The twenty-year period I spent studying and learning was what allowed me to change my vibrational level to the point of being able to hear them.

In the summer of 1983, I was in a tumultuous relationship that ended abruptly because of emotional problems between the two of us, and I was devastated. I did not understand what had happened or why he became so enraged at what I thought were totally innocent and harmless comments I occasionally made during conversations. After he left, I needed a change of scene and called my oldest and dearest friend to ask if I could visit him and his daughter, also a good friend. Of course, John said yes, and off I went to Montana. It was a place I often visited to study singing with him and to visit with his wife, Willa, and daughter, Joanna, who had introduced me to astrology many years earlier. This time she had something, or rather, *someone*, much more important to tell me about.

Joanna had always been searching for the truth, in the deepest sense of the word, and also for the best way to heal others by helping them to heal themselves. Along the way, she met Dr. Ron Scolastico, a transpersonal psychologist. Ron is a "channel" for a group of beings from beyond the Veil whom he calls the "Guides".

When I arrived in Montana, Joanna told me she had a series of five tapes of channeled material she had gotten from Ron and suggested I might want to hear a bit of the information. When I first heard Ron's voice transmitting the heartfelt messages of the Guides, I knew I had to meet him and talk with the Guides myself, and I asked Joanna where I could find him. She told me he would be in New York City in early September and gave me the telephone number of the woman who was hosting his visit there. I called her immediately and made an appointment.

On September 8, 1983, I rang the doorbell to the apartment where Ron was staying, and he opened the door. I looked into the bluest eyes I had ever seen and followed him into the study where he was holding his sessions. I noticed the box of tissues on the side table and wondered if I would need one.

After a few questions and explanations from Ron, we started. The Guides began my session with the words that would later become so familiar to me: *"We are here now and we would welcome yourself..."* and continued with their introduction. They then asked if I had questions, and I asked my first question about my purpose for being on Earth. Their response was intriguing.

My second question was the one I had originally made the appointment for, which was to discover the cause of the strange anger from my former partner. Their answer was so right, so true, that I immediately felt the inner knowing of hearing the truth, and I felt their love for me, a love that was totally unconditional and totally unknown to me at that time. I had never, in this existence upon Earth, felt such a deep, compassionate, and understanding love before. It was a wonderful feeling and one that I wanted to sink into, to simply release all my fears, all my difficulties, all my own angers. It was a love beyond Earth's boundaries and one that I wanted to feel again and again.

I returned to my apartment and played the tape over and over, feeling the beautiful and unconditional love all over again and happy to have found the root cause of the problem between my former partner and myself. The veil had been lifted from my eyes, and I could see him in a totally different light. I could feel compassion for him because I understood completely what the underlying emotions were like for him. I felt at peace with the breakup and at peace when talking with him subsequently. I never told him what I had found in my session with Ron, and I know that I chose the best solution for us. He seemed to have moved on quite happily, and I could then move on quite happily also, although I did have occasional feelings of regret that we had had to part. That said, I now can thank him from the bottom of my heart for being the catalyst he was for an enormous change in me and in my life path. Thank you, dear one, for your love *and* your anger, both of which changed my life for the better.

After this period in my life, I continued having sessions with Ron and continued having deep insights into relationships of all kinds and the causes of difficulties within them. Ron and the Guides have been a support system for me that was invaluable, and I treasure our friendship. Thank you, Ron, for all your love and assistance over the years.

After this awakening to the possibilities that lay before me, I continued by beginning to meditate. The Guides had suggested a period of five to ten minutes to begin, and that is what I did. It seemed very easy to just close my eyes and concentrate on nothing, and it helped with the stresses of my career as a dramatic soprano in the world of grand opera. I had been singing professionally since May 1967, when I made my debut during the Vienna Festival as Marietta-Marie in Korngold's *Die Tote Stadt*. This was the beginning of a way of life that would eventually take me all over the world, and I performed in the opera houses of North America, South America, Europe, Asia, and Australia over the following thirty-five years. It was a very fulfilling existence, but very, very stressful, and the meditations helped enormously. Gradually, I increased my meditations to thirty minutes and then, sometimes, to an hour. I began to have visions during my periods of stillness, and enjoyed the quiet time immensely.

Also in this period I began reading everything I could find on metaphysics, spirituality, world religions, and healing modalities. I read *The Findhorn Garden* after it fell off the shelf in front of me one day in a bookstore in Chicago. Funny, that. Then I mentioned the book to a friend, and he told me that an acquaintance of his had been to Findhorn and loved it, and that perhaps I might like it also. I wrote to them for a brochure and information packet. I carried it with me to my next job in Italy, and decided while there to apply. I sent the information off to them and within one week had a response. Unbelievable! So off to the Findhorn Community in Northern Scotland I went for the Spring Festival of the Arts.

I arrived at Inverness Airport and met with the others also arriving on my flight. We were taken up to the Findhorn Community by a group of permanent members, and there we were given our room assignments. I was to stay at the old Cluny Hotel. This was slightly disappointing, as I had hoped to be down in the original Findhorn Garden area, but of course Cluny was where I was absolutely supposed to be, as I learned later.

I had arrived a week before the Spring Festival of the Arts in order to take part in "Experience Week", and the day after we arrived, we met in our assigned groups, where a very interesting method of deciding on our tasks for the week was presented to us. Of course, most of my group wanted to work in the famous Findhorn Garden. I actually was more interested in working in the publications department. We all were instructed to close our eyes and look for some sort of indication of our "jobs" for the week. I closed my eyes, expecting to see books or pamphlets, and what appeared? A wheelbarrow! I was very surprised at this and silently asked again for an image for my job for the week. Again, a wheelbarrow!

When we were all instructed to open our eyes, the focalizer read a list of the possible jobs, and we raised our hands as the one that corresponded to the symbol we had received was read out. Of course, I raised my hand for the famous garden, along with about fifteen other people. There were only eight positions to be given out that week for work in the various gardens, so we had to do a process of "releasing". We all closed our eyes again and looked for our symbols. Again, I saw the wheelbarrow and when we were asked to raise our hands again for the gardens, I raised mine. About five of the people who thought they were to work in the gardens had released their idea of that, leaving about ten of us. Again we were asked to close our eyes and release. I again saw the wheelbarrow, so when we were asked again, I stuck my hand up, secure in the knowledge that I was to work in the gardens. Eventually, there were only eight of us who were actually meant to work in the gardens. I was not to go to the famous Garden of Findhorn, but to the garden at Cluny Hotel.

We all separated and went to our various spots to meet our focalizers for the work week. When we arrived in the Cluny garden, there was no wheelbarrow to be seen! Oh, dear. I instantly thought that perhaps I had taken someone else's spot. However, I remembered how often I had seen the wheelbarrow, and so I said nothing, trusting that I was in the right place at the right time, and we got to work, sifting through the rough soil and removing rocks so that our section of the Cluny Garden could be planted.

The next morning, I reported to work and found that we were to clear weeds out of the flowerbeds at the front of Cluny Hotel. We were instructed to go to the back of the building and bring bark chips around to the front for mulch. As we rounded the corner of the building, there was my *wheelbarrow!* I was so relieved that my visualization had been correct after all that I got to work with a vengeance, shoveling bark into the barrow and trotting around to the front with it. We had a great time, and the work was very rewarding.

On Wednesday, I was reassigned for one day to the Findhorn Press Office! It was a surprise, and I was pleased to be able to see the inner workings of the publishing arm of the Findhorn Foundation. However, I also was glad that I would be returning to the garden at Cluny the next day. We planted seedlings there on Thursday, and then I was assigned to harvest parsnips in the garden at Newbold House, a part of the wider Findhorn Foundation Community, on Good Friday. My experiences working in the gardens were magical in every way.

After the Experience Week was finished, those of us staying on were given new room assignments and a new group to join for the Spring Festival of the Arts. I remember now how pleased I was to attend a concert in the Great Hall, a beautiful new building on the original Findhorn Garden lands. And how surprised and happy I felt as the couple singing for us introduced themselves and asked this question: "Anybody here believe in reincarnation?" As I was about to raise my hand, everyone else in the auditorium laughed out loud, and I realized that I was finally a member of a group of people who all believed exactly as I believed. It was an incredibly satisfying and new sensation, and one I cherished long afterward. And of course, the answer to the question and the laughter was "Nice to see you all again."

After I left Findhorn, I continued with my singing career, reading books about spirituality, meditating in my free time, and wondering where this would take me. I decided to return to Firdhorn another time and had a period free at the end of that year. I went for another two weeks in the deepest, darkest winter and promptly became ill with a terrible lung infection that lasted the entire time I was there. I tried every healing modality at my disposal at Findhorn to heal this affliction, to no avail.

When I returned to New York City, I consulted my throat specialist and was given antibiotics for the infection. That cleared it up in about two weeks, after all the past life regression and other therapies available at Findhorn had failed to heal me. This puzzled me at the time. I now know that a tremendous belief that one *can* be healed is necessary, along with the proper technique for that healing. Once an illness has descended from the emotional or mental body into the physical body, the degree of difficulty of the healing increases exponentially. The trick is to keep the auric field clean in order to catch any negative thoughts or thought-forms that might tend to manifest as a physical illness over time. However, it took me a long, long time to reach this conclusion, and I had many throat infections and lung infections and many series of antibiotics to heal them during my time of metaphysical studies while I was still singing opera.

I write all this as an explanation of the pathway I took to reach the point in my spiritual development where I could become clear enough vibrationally, to be able to hear beings from the other side of the Veil speaking to me. It took twenty years almost exactly, from September 1983 to July 2003, and many,

many workshops, seminars, meditations, and books to bring me to this point in my life.

Sometimes I can hear the Archangels speaking quite clearly, and I simply repeat the words they say, and at other times, their messages come through me without my interfering. In these cases, I do not remember what was said, because I did not "hear" them but simply allowed the thoughts and thought-forms to flow through me in a stream of consciousness. When the message comes through in an easy, flowing way, I believe I am in a deeper state of brain wave called theta. I suspect that when I "hear" the words and repeat them aloud, I am in a state of deep alpha brain waves, which allows me to remain "conscious" of what is happening to me, in me, and around me. In the deeper state of theta, I am unaware of my surroundings, but am still *in* my body, not *out* of my body.

My connection with the Archangelic group allows me and my husband to channel their healing energies through us and into others, and also allows me to give to our clients a loving personal message from the Archangels during their healing sessions. This method of healing has brought some miraculous results for our clients, and we are gratified and happy when we receive confirmation from them of the wonderful healing work the Archangels are doing through us. I feel blessed to be able to participate in any way in another's healing, and I know my husband feels the same way. We look forward to facilitating many more healings and channelings for others and ourselves.

It is here that I wish to thank Archangel Michael for his words channeled through Ronna Herman at Lake Tahoe in October

2008. When he looked at us and said, "It is time to jump off the mountaintop. We will catch you", I knew that he meant that my self-imposed "vacation" from channeling was over. I had taken the period from February 2005 to October 2008 off to devote all my time and energy to my relationship with my new husband, Frans, but when Michael looked at me, and spoke to me, well, that was that! I began the next day to open to the Archangels again, and this book is the result.

I have received these messages from a very large group of Angelic Beings, including the Archangels we all know and love. They are solely responsible for the creation of the content of this book, which they gave me in meditation, and I refer you, dear readers, or listeners, as the case may be, to the group of Archangels themselves for answers to any questions you might have.

I welcome your comments always, and I hope that this book is beneficial for all of you. It has been for me.

Marilyn Zschau Baars, C.C.H.T., Co-director, Archangel Healing
www.archangel-healing.com/ archangelhealing@gmail.com

A NOTE TO READERS/ LISTENERS

I wish here to say a few words about the language and syntax used by the Archangels in this book.

The Archangels make it clear throughout this book that they are speaking to your hearts and they ask that you read and listen with your hearts. The words that they have spoken through me may sound archaic and stilted to some of you, and they may sound flowing and graceful to others. In any case, the manner in which they speak has its own rhythm and flow, and conforms to the language "spoken" on the other side of the Veil, which is the "Language of Light". I myself have heard this "Language of Light" spoken by a person who gifted herself with the ability to do so, and I must tell you that it is the most beautiful and moving language I have ever heard, and it brought me to tears. So please read this book without judgment and with your hearts so that you may receive the vibrations of the "Language of Light". I hope that it will be a transformational experience for all of you.

Marilyn Zschau Baars, C.C.H.T.

FOREWORD

FROM THE ARCHANGELS: THE BOOK OF THE ASCENSION

TO OUR CO-CREATORS:

We greet you now, and we would say to begin that the writing and completion of a book is good and that if you wish, we will give you the information which you can put into this book for others to read, information that will carry an energetic print, a blueprint of our energies, so that not only the reading of the book will be beneficial but holding the book will be beneficial because of the energies contained within the book from us that will emanate through the words on the pages. This will be important for you to tell ahead of time, in advance, so that those who might be wavering in their decision to purchase this book will feel that they are benefiting totally not only by reading, but also by *feeling* what is coming out of the book. We will make sure that when the pages are printed, that our energies are flowing into the paper, into the ink, into the words themselves, so that they will be able to be felt by all who hold the book in their hands and who read the material, some of which you will write as a history, and some of which, the majority of which, we will give you, information from us, information from the entire Angelic Realm, information from The Goddess, and information from The Creator of All There Is.

We wish you to begin as soon as possible with the transcribing of every message that we give you daily, and in a short time, you will have the majority of what we would like to present in this book. We suggest you consider also offering this book in an electronic format where you read the book onto a digital format that is necessary for transmission through the Internet, through your computer, through a CD, or through print. We know that this information will be in demand and the energy part of it will be at least one-half of the interest that is generated, because it will seem *magical*, and those who hold the book or listen to our speaking through you, listen to your voice reading the material, will feel different from the times in which they have heard other material recited or read other books. They will feel the energy and they will understand, once you have told everyone that this is the process that we are entering into with you as our emissaries, that you both will be representatives for us, and that Frans himself will have another project coming up that is his own and mixed with the energies of the Higher realms as well, and he understands what we are speaking of at this point.

We ask that you both begin your books as soon as possible, for time is of the essence, and the material needs to come out as soon as possible. We would suggest that you participate in these seminars that have been offered to you, because of the exposure to others of spiritual beliefs. The word will spread from them outward, gathering you an even larger audience than you have been used to seeing.

Once the book has been released, prepare yourselves for enormous changes in your lives, for once the people understand that our words have healing properties because of the energy that we infuse into them, they will want to be in your presences. They will want to be healed, all of them, and you may be able to fulfill your agreement with us, which is to bring our healing energies onto the Earth in a more accessible form for all, for all beings incarnate on this planet at this time.

There is a great need for healing: emotional healing, mental healing, spiritual healing. Many people are confused and many people are lost, or feel that they are lost, for in truth no one is ever truly lost. Even the ones who know that they are enlightened to a certain degree still have need of healing of their physical forms, of their emotional bodies, in some cases of their mental bodies, and they all will want to know you. They all will want to possess the book.

We will put the highest level of energy possible for the Earth plane into this book, in both written and oral form, so that you may send our messages out to as many individuals as possible.

We told you in the beginning: "If you will stick your neck out in the spiritual community, we will bring you the clients". And you have stuck your neck out, and you have jumped off the mountaintop, and we have caught you.

Marilyn Zschau Baars

Always know that you are safe. You are protected, no matter what Earth changes transpire; you need never fear again of the loss of your physical form. Trust in us. Believe that you are safe. Believe that you are protected. And know that we are who we say we are: WE ARE THE ARCHANGELS, *all*, and many more, unnamed, but truly existing. There are innumerable ones of us, and this may be difficult for many to believe because of the limitations placed by religious groups upon the naming and the numbering of so-called "Archangels", but we assure you there are many, many, many more than anyone could ever count. We are Infinite and we are, in a sense, One.

We come to you because of an agreement, made before you came into physical form, for you are a member of our group and we love you so very much, both of you: Our representatives in physical form, our Emissaries of Archangelic Light and Love.

So we ask you to remember this in all of your interactions with others in physical form. Remember you are representing us. Remember to keep that at the front of your minds at all times and know that even the smallest interaction with another, animal or human, has an impact on everything else through a bolt of energy within this Universe and others that are incomprehensible to those in human form. But we assure you, every action causes a reaction, and on and on and on, and the very best actions create the very best reactions.

The higher your level of energy is in interactions with others, the higher the reaction, the greater the benefit for the entire human race, the entire planet Earth, the entire Solar System, and the entire Universe.

Please remember to act from your highest point of energetic perfection at all times. Spread our Love before you wherever you go, and know that we are with you always, even in your darkest hours. We applaud you for continuing your development energetically, and we say to you that any interactions with beings of high energetic vibration are good. Know that you are safe at all times. Know that all decisions you make for yourselves are "good", in Earth terms (are "*beneficial*" in our terms), and we ask you to continue with the healing work in particular, as you have seen recently the great difference that we, and you, together can create on Earth for others.

We ask you to bear all things with good humor, to remember that the third dimension is slowly dissolving and blending into higher dimensional levels and to aim your aspirations always on The Light, on becoming The Light, on becoming higher frequency, ever higher and higher. Pull yourselves up out of the density of the third dimension, bit-by-bit, step-by-step, breath-by-breath.

We ask you to remember that you may breathe in our energies into your body at any time. Remember to pull it deeply into your heart, move it up into your head, and fill the rest of your body with our energies at all times. If you remember to do this, it will be easy for you to spread our energies around you. If you like, perhaps you could take one or two minutes at the beginning of every hour to stop what you are doing and remember to breathe our energies in, just one or two minutes, longer if you like, to focus all of your attention on your breath and our energies, pulling them in, pulling them into your bodies and healing, healing everything, one or two minutes at the beginning of every hour.

It is not very much in Earth terms, but it has an infinite benefit in universal terms.

As you come closer to us in these minutes, you come closer to us in your vibrational levels and you will more rapidly become Beings of Light, ready to operate and participate in fifth-dimensional energies of unconditional love. When you reach the point of unconditional love, you will know that you are of the vibrational level that is equivalent to the fifth dimension, and then you can become sixth-dimensional beings and seventh-dimensional beings. Breathing in our energies will rejuvenate your bodies and will help you immensely in going forth as our Emissaries of Light and Love.

We rain our Rays of Light down upon you now. Open every pore and allow them to enter your bodies, and know that you are beloved beyond all measure, that we send you our gratitude for speaking for us, for healing for us, and for living our messages yourselves.

We are the Archangels, and these are our truths forever, without end.

THE GOLDEN ESSENCE IS YOU

CHAPTER ONE

CHRISTMAS DAY, DECEMBER 25, 2009

THE FREQUENCY OF LOVE;

ARCHANGEL MEDITATION: THE JOURNEY TO THE SEA OF LIGHT AND LOVE

The Frequency of Love is as high as the highest sky and as deep as the deepest sea.

We give you these words in Earth terminology, for in truth The Frequency of Love is All There Is. It is in everything, it is everywhere, in all places, all planets, all suns, all asteroids, all universes. It is All There Is, and The Frequency of Love is in actuality the frequency of The Creator Light, of The Source. But to use these terms for many does not supply them with the more finite ideas of "What Is", and so to say that The Frequency of Love is as high as the highest sky and as deep as the deepest sea is more understandable for many, more simple, more easy to remember, to be able to repeat to one's self in quiet moments, in moments of turmoil, in moments of difficulty, in moments of peace, in moments of love. To remember "the highest sky and the deepest sea" is quite easy, but the more amorphous terminology of "Love Is All There Is" may be a bit difficult for some to grasp; even though the words *seem* simple, they are not.

The tiniest particle of life is composed of Love. The largest stone that you can imagine is composed of Love. The hottest fire is pure Love. And the coldest ice is, of course, Love. The water, the air, the fire, the rock, the plants, the grass, the trees, the birds, the breeze from the sea, the heat from the sun, the cold of arctic night, all is Love.

We wish to take you on a meditation journey now, centered around Love, and we ask that you simply listen and follow along with your beings, with your beingness, with your senses.

We ask you to use your imaginations. Those of you who find it a challenge to visualize with your eyes closed, just simply listen and we will take you with us to the most beautiful Light that you could ever hope to see.

MEDITATION:
THE JOURNEY TO THE SEA OF LIGHT AND LOVE

Take a few deep, relaxing breaths, and allow all the tensions to melt away. Feel your body relaxing into wherever it is that you are sitting. Become aware of your breath, of your lungs. Keep the breathing regular, and slow. The slow evenness of breathing is inherently relaxing and facilitates a deeper state of brain wave, leading you through the alpha brain wave state into the what is called theta state, and the theta into the delta. So if you continue to breathe slower and slower, your body and brain recognize the signals to relax, to come ever closer to the state of deep sleep, and it is in this state of deep relaxation that you may attain that state of mind which allows you to travel away from your body, away from all thoughts. It allows you to become aware of other states of relaxation and total peace and harmony, which is the state of becoming Love, not only feeling it, or sensing it, or even imagining it. It is the act of becoming, becoming Love. You may begin to sense a feeling of Light, not only of *seeing* Light, but also *feeling* Light.

Continue the very slow in-breath, and out-breath, as you allow the Light to expand. As you come closer and closer to that Light, that Light joins with you, till you merge with the Light. Feel at one with the Light, that warm Light, a soft lemon-yellow glow. And as you become the Light, you begin to merge more deeply with the Light, allowing your molecules to intermingle with the molecules of the Light, which is now becoming brighter and more white in color.

When you can sense that you are fully mingled with the pure white Light, you know that you ARE The Creator Light, that you ARE All There Is, and you merge into oneness with the pure, white shimmering Light of The Creator Source of All There Is, and you feel your heart beginning to expand more and more, opening up to allow The Creator Light to flow into your heart. You allow this Light to fill your heart because you know that the Light can heal you. Allowing the Light into your heart and expanding this Light throughout your body is more beneficial than you could ever know.

If you continue to allow the Light to enter your heart, to allow the Light to flow throughout your body, to expand the Light even further outward from your physical body, outward into your etheric body, flowing ever outward into all the other bodies, you will experience a deep, deep healing every time that you sit and allow us to guide you through this Meditation of Light and of Love from The Source of All There Is, from The Creator, shining Its Light upon you and sending it through us into your heart. You will experience the deepest peace, the highest Love, and the most profound healing possible on the Earth plane. With every word we speak to you, we bring our vibrations, which come from The Creator, into your bodies for healing.

We ask you now to become aware of the pulsing of the Light within your bodies, to tune in to that sensation of pulsing, to see the energies of the

Light pulsing in and out, in and out, in and out, so that you know The Infinite Source of Light and Love that is available to you within the pulsing.

Take a deep breath now, and imagine that pulsing filling you, filling your auric field, with every breath filling it more, causing your auric field to expand ever outward, becoming larger and larger, filling more and more with the Light of Love, filling the space around you more and more, fuller and fuller, until you are floating in The Sea of Light and Love. You can release and simply float, suspended and supported by The Sea of Love and Light. We ask you now to continue floating, as we remain silent...

(two-minute pause...)

And now, as we return to speak with you, we ask you to remember to come to this place as often as you like, and if you like, to repeat certain phrases that are helpful for the returning. We give you now a few of these, which you may use whenever you like:

The Golden Essence Is YOU

I AM
THE HIGHEST FREQUENCY
OF LOVE AND LIGHT.

I AM
ONE WITH THE SOURCE OF
ALL THERE IS.

I AM
PEACE.

I AM
LOVE.

I AM
THE DIVINE CREATOR.

And every time that you use these phrases, you will find it easier to achieve this state of relaxation, which is deep enough to be where you are now, floating in The Sea of Love.

We will now journey with you back to your full waking state, allowing you to return slowly, asking you to increase the rate of your breathing so that you come back slowly, by breathing more rapidly... in and out...in and out...in and out...in and out... in...out...in...out...so that you are more centered into your bodies, moving your feet, moving your hands, moving your arms and your head from side to side, feeling more and more into your body and slowly, slowly opening your eyes and coming back to the fully aware, fully awake state, remembering and bringing with you the feelings of complete Unconditional Love.

And we say to you: when you float in The Sea of Unconditional Love, you create a pathway for your body, your brain, your nervous system, your blood, your fluids, most especially the water, by remembering how to return to The Sea of Love.

✤✤✤

We ask you now to look around you, look at the room, see everything that you are so familiar with, or perhaps not familiar with, and know that everything you see, everything you see, is Love in physical form. You are surrounded at all times by Love, by the creations of Love, by the manifestations of Love in the third dimension.

Understand and know and realize that everything that you are able to look upon without judgment is beneficial for you because it is Love.

EVERYTHING IS LOVE.

And so we take our leave of you now. Until the next time...

We are the Archangels and more, and these are our truths this day.

CHAPTER TWO

THE WHITE, PINK, AND RED ROSES

(This session was truncated, but contains some interesting information, so I am including it for readers/listeners.)

MZB: The Archangels led me through a visualization exercise. They first asked me to visualize a white rose out in front of me and to call back all my energy...physical energy...into that white rose and see it grow and grow and grow until it becomes quite large and then, to bring that rose into the heart so the energy comes back to the physical body. Then they asked me to see a pink rose out in front and asked me to call back all the loving energies I had given away in this lifetime to anything...animal, plant, human, whatever...to see that pink rose growing larger and larger and pull it also into the heart. And then there was a red rose for all the passion energy that had ever gone into anything or anybody: any example of feelings of deep involvement of passion, of singing, of anything. They asked me to see that rose grow very large and pull it back into the heart. Let me see if they want to add anything to that...

We would say only that this exercise is extremely valuable, especially in cases where individuals are feeling depleted of energy, where they feel that they have given and given and given and have received nothing in return. When you have clients who express these feelings and have actually presented themselves as very, very tired, very, very exhausted, this is a good exercise to take them through, to bring them down, with breathing, into an altered state, and then do the visualization with them. It takes not a very long time, and it's very beneficial for people in a...caught in a "giving" situation and who feel that they are not receiving back their energy, or energies.

We would also like to say that the progress of the book may seem very slow to you, but that it is taking no time at all in reality, for it is already finished and you need only access the finished product. If, however, you prefer that we give you pieces of it, day-by-day, we can do that as well.

MZB: *"Yes, I'd like for you to do that".*

Very well. It will take a little longer to do it this way, but if that is your preference, then of course...

MZB: *Then I say, "Yes, I would like very much to feel that you are telling me everything." Apparently, I can download it through my Higher Self...*

"Yes" *they say,* "that's true".

For today we would like you to repeat the meditation exercise, which we gave you, *The Journey to the Sea of Love and Light*, and you can do that with the tape that you have. We would like for you both to do that meditation as often as you would like, for it is very beneficial in loosening up the ties that bind you to the Earth and it will, the repeating of it, will allow you to become more and more filled with The Light of Love from The Source of All There Is. The more of The Light of The Source that you receive into your bodies, the easier it will be for you to access our Light, for in truth, all is The Light of The Source; it is just that we have a specialty of working with humans to assist you on your journeys forward in growth and involvement with the coming Ascended Masters returning to the angelic fold. We see that you are both journeying together on this path and we congratulate you for your dedication to The Light.

MZB: *I'm having some trouble today hearing easily...it seems to come in spurts...*

We see that, yes, you are feeling less connected today and that is simply a...an involvement with earthly things and preoccupations...a few small worries...There are a number of reasons why you feel that the connection is not smooth today...but we say to you that of course you are always connected to us and becoming...it becomes easier with the passage of time...and then...it depends upon the depth of your [MZB: *I want to say "brain waves"—they mean the <u>frequency</u> of the brain waves...*]...the depth of meditation is important, for if you remain close to the waking state, it is of course more difficult for you to hear us. Perhaps it would be good to spend more time "tuning in" to a deeper level of brain waves...frequencies...brain wave frequencies...in the future. If you would like, you could do the meditation that we gave you now, and after that, we could speak again.

We did not receive any more of their message that day.

CHAPTER THREE

REGENERATION AND MIRACLES

"The glory of the Lord shone round about them" is written in your book called the Bible, and indeed, what was then spoken of as "the glory of the Lord" was in actual fact The Light of The Creator, which shines visibly from within all beings of high vibrational level.

Using this meditation (*The Journey to The Sea of Light and Love*) daily will bring all of you who listen to it and who use it regularly to a higher vibrational level. It will facilitate your becoming able to reach levels higher than that in which you currently reside, higher than what is commonly referred to as the third dimension, even the fourth dimension, higher than what you call the fifth dimension, so that you can become (come) closer to that level at which we exist. In order to achieve this, it is most important that you learn how to release your bodies and to float out of them, as you do at night during the deep sleep state, when your bodies are regenerating themselves and you... your...what you call "spirits" are free to leave the body behind and go to various places in what is called "the Spirit World", "the Other World", "Heaven". All of these terms refer to the higher dimensional levels above and beyond the pull of Earth's gravity. You can think of it as "outer space" if you like, but know that it is not "outer space". It is simply that you're vibrating at a different frequency, more rapidly, much more rapidly than the third dimension or the fourth and, in some ways, even the fifth. There are many levels in each dimension that are separately attainable, depending on your vibrational frequency. In order to move from one level to another, you need only change your vibrational frequency, either faster or slower. Faster, of course, are the frequencies closer to the Angelic Realm, closer to the so-called "Higher Realms" but that are in actuality simply of a faster vibration.

The main reason that you beings on Earth are unable to see us is simply a matter of different vibrational frequencies. If you can attain a higher vibrational frequency, then you can see us, if that is your desire. In fact, there are many upon the Earth now who are able to see us, for they have raised their vibrations to the point at which they can "see" when we lower our vibrations in order to be in the third and fourth dimensions. So it is not necessarily true that they are of our vibratory level, because we must lower our vibrational level in order to reach you. But they are of a higher vibrational level than most humans, and therefore are able to see the manifestation of us that we arrange for you to see.

Those of you who do not see, do not be discouraged, for it is simply a matter of learning to look a bit more freely than usual. It is a matter of clearing the channel between you and us and other Beings of high vibrational levels, some of whom you refer to as "Aliens". They too can lower their vibrational levels to the point where they are visible, but this is not a common occurrence, since it consumes a great deal of energy to change one's vibrational level back to a higher state while conscious. To change the state of the vibrational frequency while unconscious, that is, while the body is unconscious, is extremely easy. It involves only exiting the body and leaving it behind, for all of you are able to do this while you are in human form. You simply allow the body to sleep and you leave.

It is important for you to know that if you state to yourself before you go to sleep at night, before you put your body to sleep, if you state your intentions for that body, you may cause changes in the cellular structure during sleep, for the brain listens to everything that you say, and the brain causes the changes to happen, if the proper circumstances are available.

The brain needs energy in order to make the changes. If you are consuming a diet that is beneficial for the body, and that has and contains the optimum ingredients for changing the body, in cases of illness, for example, it is important that you pay close attention to the foods that you consume, both when completely healthy, and, more importantly, when *not* completely healthy, or when you are ill.

If you express aloud to yourself what it is that you wish the brain to accomplish for the body before you sleep, and the conditions are right and the belief system is in place that will allow for the changes to be made, know that every effort possible will be made by the brain to comply with your request. This is a process which is available to all of you, but one about which little, if anything, is known, for, because of the agreement made before you came into physical form, and the Veil, which is still largely in place, you have not had access to this information until now.

Know that the intention, the anticipation of wellness, the belief that the body is capable of healing itself, and the addition of loving energy from The Source of All There Is, in addition to the proper nutrients and the expressed desire for the brain to heal the body during sleep, these are all the things that must be in alignment before a so-called "miracle healing" can take place. Of all the ingredients of a miracle healing, the most important is the *belief* that it is possible. All the other ingredients can be in place, but if there is no deep-seated belief in miracles, none will occur, for the human will continue to sit in its negative expectations and its belief that others know better, and in its belief that healing is not possible.

There are many, many negative thoughts that can interfere with a miracle healing, and we say to you now that miracles are indeed possible, they are attainable, they are there for you to access. You need only combine all of the ingredients that we have expressed with the belief that miracles are possible. *Believe* that the brain can reverse any negative trend in the cells of the body. The brain can change any situation that may seem hopeless, but you *must believe* that it is possible. You must believe that the brain is that powerful.

The brain's purpose, the brain's *main* purpose, is to heal your body, and whatever you feed your brain, be it nutrients which you ingest, or thoughts that keep recurring, you must know that everything you think and everything you say, everything you drink, and everything you eat affects the health of your brain. The air you breathe affects your brain. The fluids you take in, or do not take in, affect your brain. If you ingest drugs, they affect your brain. Everything affects your brain. And your brain is the control center for all of the cells of your body.

The brain is the control center for your entire body. Do whatever you need to do in order to change your thinking, if necessary, for it is your thoughts that hinder you. It is your beliefs that hold you back, if they are not completely positive, and it is all of the substances that you ingest that either heal you or cause you pain, difficulties, illnesses, and even premature death of the body.

The most important thing that you can do for your body is to give it all of the nutrients that it needs, and fill it daily with The Light of Love from The Source of All There Is.

We recommend for any being in physical distress that they stop during their day for a few moments, take a breathing break, slow their breathing down, and imagine themselves floating in the Sea of Love and Light of The Creator Source of All There Is. Know that even only a few moments of imagining and feeling your body relaxing and floating in The Light, your molecules intermingling with The Light, only a few moments, are more beneficial than you can possibly imagine. If you follow our suggestions, you will attain a higher level of beneficial vibrations for your human body, so that you can lead it to the point of allowing it to regenerate itself at night, without your suggestions of what to do given to the brain. You may turn your body over to your brain, and your brain will know what to do.

Spend the last few moments before sleep floating in The Sea of Love and Light of The Creator Source of All There Is. This will prepare your body for the most restful and regenerative sleep possible, and it will allow you to more easily attain a higher level of vibrational rate as you leave your body. Remember and know that you are always safe when you are out of your body, that your body is protected, that you are connected to your body and will always return to it. Most humans do not journey very far, but come to a level of teaching and learning which we will not speak of now, for this information we are giving you today concerns the health of the human body, and not the adventures of the Soul Part, which leaves in the night and returns again to live another day upon the Earth in the beauty of the glorious creation in which you all took part in the beginning.

So we say to you now: Look to your belief systems, look to your dietary matters, when you wish to effect a healing of the physical form and when you wish to maintain your physical form in optimal health. Be happy. Be joyful. Be positive in all ways. Create for yourselves upon the Earth the most beautiful physical form which serves your needs and which maintains your journey upon the Earth until that point at which you wish to leave the Earth and return Home to The Source, to The Creator, to The Love, greater than any love you have ever known upon the Earth, the all-encompassing, judgment-free, always-accepting Love of The Source, of your Creator, of The Mighty All There Is.

We are the Archangels this day and always, and these are our truths.

CHAPTER FOUR

THE CREATOR'S LOVE AND LIGHT; AGREEMENTS

We would like to continue with more information for you from The Book of Energy *(this book's working title)*.

The Energy of Love, the Frequency of Love, and The Light of All There Is comes to you in a continuous stream, unbroken and unending, and whether or not you recognize it for what it is, and feel its vibrational frequency, is dependent upon the level of awareness that you can achieve separate from your day-to-day existence upon planet Earth. Some of you are born with gifts that allow you to feel energies more than others, and some of you learn how to feel the energies. It is very important that you understand that no matter whether you are aware of the energies or not, they are continually streaming into you, into your bodies, around you, above you, below you. They are always available for you at all times. Whether or not you choose to use them for *directed purpose* is up to you.

You are sustained by the air you breathe, by the light you feel, by the water you drink, and by the foods you ingest, but we tell you now that were this energy from The Source of All There Is to stop flowing towards you, you would no longer exist. And so we offer you the reassurance that the Light, the Love, and the energy is unending. It continues forever. The Creator expands and expands and expands, sending Its energy out in waves of Light and Love that come to you in greater or lesser amounts, depending upon certain parameters which are natural and which we may discuss at a later period.

We wish you to know now, today, that the most important thing about life anywhere is the reception of The Creator Love, The Creator Light, The Essence of All There Is. This is what sustains you, this is what sustains us, this is what sustains the physical universe, this is what sustains the invisible universes, this is what sustains everything, and it is unending. It continually flows in all directions outward from that great Point of Light we all call The Great Sun.

The Great Sun *is* The Creator Light. The Great Sun sustains all life and The Great Sun sustains your life, and when you journey to The Sea of Life, of Love, of Light, you are even more renewed in your physical form, for you are immersing yourselves in The Essence of The Creator consciously. You are consciously asking to have The Creator Light permeate your beings, to flow even more fully into you, to bring you better health, a greater understanding of your place in the universe and your place upon the Earth, along with all those who inhabit this Earth space along with you.

You will see in the coming year (2010) many changes happening upon your Earth, and we wish to assure you that those of you who continue to fill yourselves more and more with The Creator Love, with The Creator Light, and who are thereby raising your vibrations to an even higher level of Light and vibratory frequency, that you will be able to withstand any challenge which comes to you on the physical level.

And if you wish, you will be able to explain to others about the changes happening upon your beloved planet Gaia, the Earth, for Gaia is also changing, as you are changing, physically. Your changes may be more disruptive for you than you feel are happening around you, or they may be not at all disruptive, and you may feel that the changes in Gaia are, in a way, terrifying for some and understandable for others.

If you can understand that the changes in the Earth, in Gaia, are necessary for her to ascend to a higher level of vibration, to a higher level of Light, then you can understand the need for what seem to be disastrous occurrences. We wish to assure all of you that the disasters, so-called, are necessary for many reasons, and we wish also to inform you that they are planned with the consent of those in physical form who participate in them. Although they may not be aware of the agreement in the physical form, all have agreed to participate in everything that happens to your planet in the coming years of Earth time. There are many instances in which the occurrences will seem overpowering. You have already experienced some of these overpoweringly disastrous occurrences in your recent time, and you have also seen the recovery after the fact, which is also a part of the agreement of the beings living in the areas where the disasters occur.

Certain Souls have made agreements with their humans to bring the humans Home, to bring their Soul Parts back with the experience of the disaster embedded in the Soul as a permanent record of what that particular part of Earth Ascension was like.

We *urge* you to remain centered, to remain calm in the face of prospective Earth changes, for those of you who have made agreements to return back to this side of the Veil will be greatly honored and welcomed with great cheering and enthusiasm from those on this side and those who accompany you. You will all congratulate one another, and you will know that you have participated in a great adventure, and you will realize yet again that you are Eternal Beings of Light who were temporarily encased in a package of earthly form of flesh and blood.

And we urge you to remember that the dropping, or the loss, of the earthly physical form is an entryway back to The Creator, to The Light, to the deepest Love you can possibly imagine, to the wonders of being a Being of Light, to the instant manifestation of your heart-felt desires.

And also we tell you that some of you will be returning Home in order to return to Earth, not immediately, but at that time when it will be necessary for many of you to return in order to establish The Era of Peace, which is coming to the Earth: The Era of Peaceful Coexistence, The Age of Love, The Age of Enlightenment, The Time of Cooperation, and The Time of Understanding All There Is and The Creation of Everything.

So we say to you now that we understand fully the depths of fear available to humans, whether instinctive or taught, and that our deepest Love flows forth to you and into your hearts, if you will allow it. Our understanding and our compassion are yours. We congratulate you for your courage, your willingness to participate in this grand adventure coming to planet Earth now, and we say to you that you are greatly loved, greatly loved. And we send you our blessings, our Love, our Light, and our healing energies through our Emissaries to you. Our energies, our Light, and our Love are always available to those of you who ask.

Remember always the universal law: *Ask for whatever it is that you wish to have.* We are not allowed to interfere in your Life Plan. We are not allowed to tell you what to do. We are not allowed to heal you. We are not allowed *anything* without your specific request. You *must* ask for our help, and we always, always, to the greatest extent possible, give to you that which you request.

We send you our Love, and our blessings this day and always.

We are the Archangels, and these are our truths.

CHAPTER FIVE

CORDS OF ATTACHMENT
AND
HOW TO RELEASE THEM

We would like to speak today of the cording which exists between humans and the process of releasing cording so that you may be free of others' energies, which may either be feeding energy *into* your body and auric field or *removing* energy from your body and field. It is most important for the Ascension Process that you all very carefully remove the ties that bind you to others. Remove and eliminate the cords that attach to yourself and to others, and the process for the removal can be complex if there are a great number of cords.

The *intention* to remove is primary and must first be in place. You must also desire to stop the connection on the levels that are draining to you. There are some who maintain that keeping the heart connection is important, and we leave that to your discretion, but in some cases, it is better to cut all of the cords, including the heart connections, and we will explain more about that later.

The first thing that you must know about cording is that every time you come in contact with another being, if there is a mutual attraction, or even a one-sided attraction, on an energetic level, the energetic field of one body sends out a "feeler" to ascertain if a cord could be connected. If the "feeler" receives a "yes" indication, then the cord is established. If there is a "no" coming out, there can be no cord connection, and we will explain more about that aspect in a moment.

When the cord is attached, it is usual for it to attach to the lower chakras. If the relationship is an intimate and sexual connection, there will be cords in the second and the third chakras. And if there is a heart connection, there will be a cord to the fourth chakra as well, to the heart. In most cases, the cords are in these three areas, but there can be other permutations of cording which connect in more complex ways.

The first thing you must do in order to release a cord is to express for yourself that you desire to sever the cording, return the energies of the other to them, and pull back into yourself your energies. It is best that you take time for this exercise of removing cording.

Sit in a quiet place where you are not disturbed, visualize the other person, see them standing before you, and speak to them to ask permission to release the cords. In case of a negative response, that is, from someone who does *not* wish to release the cords, move to the Higher Self level of both of you, and ask your Higher Self to receive permission from the Higher Self of the other to cut the connections. In almost all cases, permission will be given, and when you receive the permission from the Higher Self, convey this to the other person, such as "I have received permission to sever these cords from your Higher Self". The person may or may not seem surprised, but they *must* agree on the Earth level, if the Higher Self has agreed.

You then take either your physical hand or an imaginary hand and imagine that you have either a scissors or a knife, a very sharp knife, in your hand. If you would like to make it a golden color, that is quite wonderful. Imagine the golden knife or the golden scissors in your hand, reach out in front of you, see the cord or cords, and with a rapid movement, sever the cords, saying as you do so:

> "I now release your energies back to you, and I bring my own energies back to myself. I wish you well, and send you Light, Love, and Peace."

As you see the cut cord in front of you — your own cord —, bring that energy back into yourself, and then pull that cord out from your body and dispose of it, in a downward motion, because the origin of a cord from someone else still contains a small particle of their energy, and you do not wish to bring that energy into your body.

This is a part of cord-cutting that is not usually recognized, or attended to, and sometimes those cutting the cords still feel an attachment to the other person. Indeed, that is because of the small amount of the other person's energy which has been brought into the body of the human cutting the cord. *It is absolutely necessary to remove that cord from your chakra.* Pull it out by its roots, and dispose of it. Mother Earth will take care of it.

Know also that you need to ask permission of others into whom you have set your cords, to remove them. And in those cases, you visualize the person standing in front of you, see the cord (or cords) that you have sent into them, ask permission to remove the cord (or cords), and then follow the same procedure to ask the Higher Self, if there is a negative response from the other human.

In cases where *you* have placed *your* cord into someone else, it is best not to cut the cord, but to reach out and pull it away, gently, from the other person, allowing their energy to exit the cord as you pull it closer to yourself. See their energy flowing back into them, out of the cord.

Wait until all of the energy is gone, then reach up and pull *that* cord out of *yourself.* Wrap it into a golden ball and give it to Mother Earth.

> The process of cord removal and cord-cutting is extremely important for the Ascension, for if you do not release all of the cords, and call all of your own energy back into you, it will not be possible for you to ascend.

Perhaps it would be good to take pen and paper, and make a list of everyone in your life with whom you have had more than a casual acquaintanceship. This list may be quite long; however, we ask you to do this as soon as possible, and we would begin with the parents, with sisters and brothers, with close childhood friendships, with teachers, and continue from there. This is especially important for your growth and your continuation toward the Ascension. We cannot urge you strongly enough to begin this process as soon as possible. Begin with your parents, your siblings, and allow this day to be the day that you are finally released from all past ties of your childhood and years until you left the fold. We recommend also cutting cords with the grandparents and any aunts and uncles, cousins, nephews, nieces — everyone in your immediate family — before you begin to cut cords with others outside of your bloodline.

When you have made your list and begun your removal of cords and cutting of cords, and after it is complete, or you believe that you have completed your cutting, we ask that you visualize your Higher Self standing in front of you, and you ask your Higher Self to hold before it a mirror in which you can see yourself on the *inner planes*. And we ask you that if you see that there are still cords, you confer with your Higher Self as to who that person is, and ask the person to step forward.

There may be in your lifetime beings you may have forgotten about, but with whom you have a cording situation. We ask you not to use a "blanket" list, but to cut these cords one-by-one, individual-by-individual, removing your cording as we have explained and cutting the cords of others. For, if you attempt to *remove* (that is, *pull* them out) the cords of others, there is the possibility that they may send more energy into you or pull more energy from you, which will make it impossible for you to pull their cord out of your chakra system. In those cases, it is best to cut the cord in the middle, as we have explained, with the golden implement, and then remove their cord from your energetic system, disposing of it as we have explained.

We wish you to understand that we know the process may become tiresome, but we assure you that when it is finished, you will be astonished at the feeling of cleanliness which fills your being and the feeling of lightness that returns to you. You will no longer feel the heaviness of being pulled backward by strings attached to you by others, and you will be free to move forward on your path, clear in the knowledge that you have done everything necessary to move forward through the Ascension Process. The time is coming when all will proceed more rapidly than you can imagine. It is time to clean up. It is time to be prepared. It is time to be free, to be able to fly, to be able to soar, to be able to meet your destiny as that Being of Light and Love you know you are.

We transmit our Love and Light to you in an unbroken stream, and we ask that you open your hearts as wide as possible in order to receive it. We are always with you, even when you don't sense it. So know that all you need do in order to receive our energies is ask. We are here, we are ready, we are willing, and we are able.

We are the Archangels, and these are our truths this day and always.

CHAPTER SIX

INSTRUCTIONS FOR ASCENSION; SIMULTANEOUS TIME; ENERGY INFUSION

We would like to discuss today the difference between waking and sleeping.

Of course, we understand that you are aware that when the body is awake, your brain-waves are of a different wavelength than when you are asleep. But we wish to speak about the becoming "awake" in the sense of becoming aware of the differences between a human who is "asleep" while awake, that is, the human is not aware, because of the Veil, of the reality of his or her true existence as an Eternal Being of Light and

Love. These humans seem to us to be asleep, for in truth, they are not awake. They are the humans who are not awake, but who are sleeping, in the sense that they are as yet unaware of their Eternal Beingness, and for those who are by chance holding this book, feeling these energies, or hearing these words, it is time now for you to wake up.

We say to you:

> OPEN YOUR ETERNAL EYES AND SEE
> THE MAGNIFICENCE OF YOUR TRUE SELF.

And to those of you who are already awake:

> OPEN YOUR EYES EVEN WIDER, AND SEE
> THE GREATNESS,
> THE MAJESTY, THE BEAUTY AND
> THE MAGNIFICENCE OF YOUR TRUE SELVES.

Know that you are capable beyond your wildest dreams, that you are honored by all of us on this side of what remains of the Veil. The Veil is thinning now, and soon you will all become aware of the truth behind your bones, your blood, your flesh, beyond your bodies, but also within your bodies:

> YOU EXIST AS ENERGETIC BEINGS
> OF LIGHT AND LOVE.

You need only remember the freedom that you feel when you are out of your bodies at night, during the sleep state of the body, which regenerates itself at night. When you leave your body behind at night, and you *all* do, you journey away from that which holds you back from returning to this side of the Veil permanently and leaving your body behind.

The Veil was put in place, and we speak of the Veil as that invisible barrier that causes the mind to forget what it was like before you inhabited the body and what it will be like when you leave the body behind and return to this side of the Veil.

We know that many of you still have fears surrounding the dying process of the body, but we say to you now that if you can, rearrange your thinking to see the dying process as a birthing process, and know that when you exit the body you are being reborn into your Soul Self and are just leaving that body behind for those molecules to return to the Earth.

Your true essence is eternal. Your true self lives forever, for you are born from The Creator Light and you are and will always remain a part of The Creator, a brilliant spark of Light, eternal energy from The Source of All There Is. You are living the experience of The Creator in human form. You have been asked to do this, and your response is always "Yes!" You have many, many experiences already behind you, and most of you will have many experiences before you, that is, in your what you call on Earth "Future".

In truth, time does not exist. Simultaneity is the time of the universe. Everything happens at once, but when you are in human form, and on the other side of the Veil, which will in future become unnecessary, you agree not to be consciously aware of all the other existences that you and your soul are experiencing in simultaneous time.

It is an agreement that has been necessary up until now, speaking in Earth terms, because you all know that if you could remember and feel again what it feels like to be out of the body, and go back into your true form of Energetic Light, you would all desire to return to what you call "Home", but what we experience as "Complete Love". The desire to be Love again is so great that none of you would wish to remain upon planet Earth, most especially within the constraints of the three dimensions that you have been experiencing, and the fourth, of which most are becoming aware.

We assure you that the time, in Earth terms, of being able to feel something similar to the unending Love that we feel is coming to Earth soon, and those of you who have prepared yourselves for what is called the "Ascension Into Light and Love" will be able to experience that in an altered form, a form which may *seem* human but which will have lost those parts of being human which have prevented you in the past from experiencing the true unconditional love which awaits you.

It is very important that you cut the cords that hold you, or tie you, to others in human form, for there will be some who will not be able to ascend, and they would hold you back with them. It is also important to meditate daily upon The Light and The Love. It is important to *expect* the changes that are coming. It is important to welcome the changes. It is important to anticipate the changes with joy — to look forward to the Ascension with joy, with radiance, with love, for those are only a few of the attributes that await you. If you have not experienced these states of being, we assure you that you will experience them after the Ascension Process is complete.

We wish also to say that we are always available to those of you who call upon us for our aid, who call upon us for help, who call upon us for advice, who call upon us for energy, who call upon us for love. Remember that you *must ask* for anything that you wish us to help you with.

Remember to drink the water, for the water is very important for the changing of the body's cells, for the mutation of the cells as they change and become lighter, more filled with Light, more filled with Love, more filled with The Creator Essence. Your bodies will be changing, gradually, and it is very important that you become aware of this now, for the Ascension is coming, and you are *in* the process now, and you must do everything possible to make it easier for your bodies to change from heaviness to lightness, from the old to the new.

We ask you now to remain steadfast in your desire to change, in your desire to fulfill your destiny, for the changes are coming and you came specifically to Earth during this period in order to experience the first Ascension without destruction of the entire planet. It is a great experiment, and it will succeed. You must see it now as already accomplished. See the end result of total joy, total happiness, total peace, total light, total beauty. Place the visualization into your expectations and ignore the rest. Ignore the negativity. Ignore the tensions. Ignore the fighting. Ignore destruction. Know that everything is changing for those of you willing, able, and ready to change.

We ask you now to take a few deep breaths while we give you an energy infusion of our Love for *all* of you. Feel the Love as it enters your heart and flows throughout your body in an unending stream of our special Angelic Energies. We say to you that we welcome this opportunity to share our energies of Love with your energies of love. We warn you that these feelings of Love can become addictive and that you might wish to sit and receive our Love over and over and over again and again, and we also say to you that this is good. It will help you to change your bodies, and you must remember to maintain a level of groundedness upon the Earth which will keep you centered and able to carry on with your daily lives without completely losing your focus for the reasons that you agreed to be upon the Earth at this time.

So take in our Love now and store it up within your hearts where you may access it at any time, especially in times when it may not be possible for you to sit quietly as you are now and receive our Love directly from us. Know that you have a storehouse of our Love within your hearts that you can call upon at any time. It is always there for you, it is always available for you to access, and, if you desire, and you express this desire, we will replenish the Love continually. You need only *ask* for whatever it is that you desire.

We leave you now and we urge you to continue with your preparations for the Shift in Consciousness towards the Ascension.

We are the Archangels, and these are our truths for this day upon the Earth. And So It Is.

CHAPTER SEVEN

THE ASCENSION; RAISING YOUR VIBRATIONAL LEVEL; ABOUT THE AFFIRMATIONS

We would like to say to begin that the time you spend tuning in to higher vibratory levels of existence magnifies and amplifies the vibrations of your own energy system. By energy system, we mean all the parts of you which are composed of energy, and the energy systems of each of you upon this planet are being asked now to step up your vibratory rates in order to be able to assimilate the energies which are now being sent to planet Earth from The Creator Source of All There Is. These energies are progressively of a higher vibration, of a higher vibratory level, than you are accustomed to feeling upon Planet Earth, and it is now imperative that you ALL do everything that you possibly can to speed up the rate of your own vibratory levels. Meditating with us is one of the ways in which you can accomplish this on a daily basis, becoming slowly faster and faster in your vibrations, in order to be able to access the higher dimensional levels as they become available to you.

And so, if you are not meditating daily, it is good to begin now in order to "catch up", so to speak, with the energies, for if you do not, it will become more and more difficult for you to exist upon this planet, as the energies will be perceived as extremely irritating to the physical body, and the energy bodies of the human will become disarrayed, or interrupted. There will be conflicting feelings, there will be short tempers, there will be many things happening within and around the human physical form that are perhaps becoming incomprehensible to those experiencing them, but which are very comprehensible to those of you who already are aware of the path that the Earth is taking at this time.

It is important for you all to know that you all must "step up to the plate", so to speak, and raise your vibratory levels, each of you, and one of the best ways of being able to do this is to cut the cords of attachment about which we spoke earlier. It is imperative that everyone begin cutting these cords as soon as possible, and continue on until all of the cords attached to you by others, or which you have attached to others, are removed, in order for you to assimilate the new energies and to use them in the most progressive and positive manner. It is very important for all of you, and especially for you who are called "Lightworkers" and who are more aware than those who may still be in the somnolent state, or a "waking/sleeping" state, that is. You may be in an "awake" state as opposed to a "sleeping" state at night, but you are not "awake" in the sense of being aware of your place in the Universe, and knowing that vibrational levels within the human body must be raised before the Ascension can happen.

For those of you who are aware of the Ascension, for those of you who are not aware of the Ascension, believe us when we tell you that a process is happening upon the Earth now which is called "The Ascension" and it is a process that the planet itself is moving through, and therefore everyone upon this planet must either move through the Ascension with the planet Gaia, or leave the planet.

This may sound quite drastic to many of you, but it is in truth simply a "coming Home" for those of you who have decided that it is not in your best interests to attempt to raise the vibrations of your physical bodies and to raise the vibrations of your energy bodies thereby. It is that many of you will feel, on an unconscious level, that it is time for you to return Home to this side of the Veil, so that you may prepare yourselves for the process of raising your vibratory levels on this side of the Veil in order to come back to Earth as a new human being of already high vibrational level, so that you may interact with those who have decided to stay and move along with the Gaia Goddess through her process of Ascension into a higher realm of vibratory rate.

This raising of the vibrational level is simply a matter of concentration, application, attention, intention, and working with Beings on this side of the Veil, be it us as the Archangels, or the Ascended Masters, the Council of Light, or any of the other Angelic Realms which you may be able to access, but we say that unless your vibratory level is extremely high already, you would not be able to reach the Seraphim or the Cherubim.

We say to you now that the process of raising the vibratory level is most important for those of you wishing to ascend, and, as we have mentioned, the cutting of the cords is imperative. Without the cutting of the cords, you may not be able to raise your vibrational level to a high enough frequency to ascend with everyone else who is ascending.

Some of you have already ascended and you are aware of what has been necessary. Some of you already were at a very high vibrational level and have not had the need to work hard to raise your vibrational level slightly. It is simply a matter of becoming aware of the necessity for all of you to join the group of souls who are now ascending and who will be ascending in the "near future" in Earth terms, as you call the "what comes next" in your lives "the future". Actually, everything is in a "NOW" Time, but that is a subject for another speaking.

So we urge you now to use our meditation that we have given you. Go to "The Sea of Love and Light" daily, more often if you wish, and you have the time and the opportunity to do so. Call upon us to help you with the process of raising your vibrations and we will be with you, of course, at all times.

We remind you that you need to *ask* us for our help at all times, and that we are available at all times and all places. It is possible

The Golden Essence Is YOU

for us to be "here" and "there" at the same time, which is a process difficult for humans to understand, but certainly not impossible for those of you on this side of the Veil, for you know the process of being "everywhere" at once. And because we can be everywhere at once, all of you may call upon us at all times, day or night. We are here, ready to attend to your call, and we are ready to help you with any process that you may be having difficulty with, be it the cord-cutting, the meditating, or anything else. The healing of the body, for example, is an important part of our service to humans.

We need for you to know that we are here for you to call upon us at all times and all places for any reason whatsoever. And if it is within your Soul Contract that we help you to heal yourself or that we help you with anything to do with your physical body, we will do so.

You must all realize that you have made "Contracts with your Soul" before you were sent to Earth by your Soul, which remains on this side of the Veil, infusing your physical body with some of its energy. The souls are extremely large, full of a very high rate of vibrational frequency, and it would be extremely difficult for a soul to totally incarnate into a physical body at this time. It is almost impossible. We are not saying that it is totally impossible, but *almost* impossible.

There are some beings upon this planet who have incarnated totally with their Soul Essence, and you would call these "Ascended Masters in human form", ready to apply their full knowledge of all lifetimes upon the Earth and elsewhere to their stated goals of being upon the Earth in order to work with humans, to help humans, and to be an example of what is possible. These would include what you call your "Avatars", for example, the Dalai Lama and Sai Baba, Babaji, who is not so visible to those of you not familiar with him, or *(who are)* not in the physical places where he appears to humans with whom he is in contact, but you know of the other two and you are aware of them and their teachings. If you are not, they *(their teachings)* are readily available in printed form.

Coming back to what we were speaking of, the vibrational frequencies of Love and Light are of the highest level that you may attain here on the Earth at this time. And so the meditation we have given you of journeying to "*The Sea of Love and Light*" can be very valuable for those of you willing and able to undertake this journey. Do not be discouraged if you do not feel that you are accomplishing anything by listening to us guide you through this meditation. You *are*. It is sometimes hidden from you.

Your accelerated learning is quite visible to us, even if you feel nothing is happening. It is happening. Make sure that you trust in the process, and that you believe in yourself, and in us, and in The Creator, and in The Creator's ability to move your energy simply by visualization. If you do not feel anything, it does not mean that you are not accomplishing something. You *are*.

Maintain your level of trust and belief in the knowledge that all is well with you in your world and that you will be changing every time you listen to this meditation, not the least of all because we have infused the method with which you hear us speaking with our energies, and every time you come into contact with our energies, we are transmitting the energies of The Creator Source of All There Is.

We are a conduit for The Source. You may always contact us in order to connect to The Source directly. If you are able to connect directly to The Source, that is wonderful for you. But those of you who have a feeling of being cut off, or not able, we ask you to release these feelings of negativity as much as possible when you enter into the meditative state. Allow them to go away into a place where you may revisit them, if you feel the need, but make sure that you drop all of your negative feelings and negative thoughts when you go into meditation; otherwise, you will carry them with you, and they *will* hold you back. If you surround yourself with a cloud of dark negativity, it is, as you may assume, more difficult to tune in to our vibrational level. It is not difficult for the Light to penetrate the darkness of the negativity, but it is difficult for *you* to imagine that that is possible. And so we ask you to put these dark feelings and dark thoughts aside for the short period of Earth time that you are with us and with The Source in "*The Meditation of Love and Light*".

We ask you now to remember also to repeat the...what you call "Affirmations" we have given you, for they are also important because they have been infused with our energies and with The Creator Light. When you say aloud, "I AM THE HIGHEST FREQUENCY OF LOVE AND LIGHT", it is true. When you say aloud, "I AM PEACE", it is true.

And so we urge you to use these affirmations before the meditation and also, if you have no time for the meditation, use them during your day to remind you. Find a quiet place and say these words aloud, for the voicing, the vocalization of the "I AM" phrase is most important, since it is heard by all parts of you. If you repeat it only silently, to yourself, it remains in a thought-form, and is not absorbed completely by the entire body. It is very important for you to repeat them aloud, and to be in a space of quietness when you do so. You may share these words with others if you wish, but we say to you that having them in the form that we are now giving them to you with our vibrations within the voice of this being speaking for us... the vibrations that we put into her voice are *most* important for the usage of the affirmations.

You may have them on a physical card, and when these cards are printed into reality on the Earth, when you have these cards, they will also be imprinted with our energies, and with the energies of The Source of All There Is. So rest assured that you *will* have in your possession physical manifestations of our energies and of the energies of The Source of All There Is. They will be in a most beautiful format for you to look upon, and we are giving our speaker now a visual form of these cards so that she may understand what it is that we are speaking of. She will find the person or persons who will print these cards.

And so now we take our leave for today, sending you an extra burst of Love and Light from The Source of All There Is.

We enwrap you in our Love. We enfold you in our Love, and our Light as well, and we send you Peace, and Blessings always.

We are the Archangels this day and always, and these speakings are our truths.

CHAPTER EIGHT

THE ASCENSION VIBRATORY LEVEL; ADDITIONAL CORD-CUTTING INFORMATION

It is time today for us to speak to you of many other things related to the information we have given you thus far, and, to begin, we would like to mention that all of the information so far has been given with the intention of bringing those of you who are reading this material, or listening to this material, up to speed, so to speak, in line with information that has perhaps already been assimilated by many of you who may be reading or seeing or hearing this information in a different format — perhaps on paper, perhaps in an audio file, or perhaps on a digital reading device.

In any case, we would like to welcome all of you to this portion of these speakings, which will begin to contain information of a more esoteric sort, and which may be a bit upsetting for some and interesting for others. We ask you to simply be with us and read and listen with your hearts, for the information that we give is always meant to be absorbed by the heart, and, to a lesser extent, by the brain, but in general, we speak to the hearts of all.

We come to you today to talk about the contacts between you on the Earth plane and those of us on this side of the so-called Veil — on this side of what can be construed as a barrier by some of you between humans and what are generally termed "spirits". We would like you to know that we are so much more than the "spirits" that you imagine, and we wish you to know that this side contains only Love. There are no conflicts this side of the Veil. There are no wars, no disruptions; nothing of a negative nature is on this side of the Veil. Everything here is of a positive nature. Everything here is created by, with, and through the expression of the Love Energy of The Creator Source of All There Is.

On this side of the Veil, it is possible for you, when you arrive here, and after you have taken the — what you would conceive of as "time" but which we know only as "experiences" — after you have experienced, or have taken the time, to consult with your Guides, your Counselors, you will begin your new accomplishments-to-be on this side of the Veil.

We wish you to know that creation is instantaneous here, and those of you who have not yet mastered the principles of creation and whose thoughts are uncontrolled, will find everything a bit chaotic after you begin creating for yourself. There will be those of us here to help you with this, and to show you how it is done, until you remember, for you have *all* experienced this before. It is just the first period after the return to this side of the Veil that those of you may be very confused. We say to you that after you have been here for a while, then you will understand, and be able to re-master, so to speak, the concepts and the process of creation here.

You will all choose what it is that you wish to accomplish for yourselves when out of form, either the physical, human form upon the Earth, or other forms, be it frequencies of energy, or other vibrational forms of a quasi-physical nature, which are difficult to explain in Earth words. There are many possibilities for your accomplishments on this side of the Veil, and you work with your counselors on this side to decide, *and* with your — "Soul Group" probably is the best term for it, — but sometimes you deal with beings who are...and we don't mean, "deal with", we mean you..."work" is not the correct word...nothing is "work" here...nothing is work on this side of the Veil, everything is joy, so we might use "joy" as a word to say that you "joy" with others from outside of your particular Soul Group also, in planning visits to other places, other galaxies, other planets, in addition to planning re-visits to planet Earth. It is all very, very complex, and very, very joyous.

It has no element of "work" associated with it, but the term "work" has been applied by so many of you for so long upon the Earth, that it is almost impossible to offer you another word, but we will use "joy" as a verb in this case, so that you can know that you joyously "joy" with other beings, other souls here, other discarnate, out-of-body beings with whom you have had long, long, long relationships on this side of the Veil, some of whom you have not met in your most recent Earth period in physical form, but whom you know and rejoice to see again, once you have come back to this side.

So we say that the preparations for continued "joy" or joyousness on this side of the Veil are endless and the possibilities are endless, and it is, as we have indicated, almost impossible to describe what it is like here, other than to say that you have, some of you have, a better idea than others. To call it "more colorful" here is not to do it justice in the sense of describing the magnificence, the beauty, the eloquence, the endless variety of colors, some of which do not even exist upon the Earth, and the variety of sounds which you cannot hear upon the Earth, but which are audible to you here, the feelings, the tasting — if you wish to *taste* something, you need only create it and it is there.

It is a wondrous, beautiful, magnificent, and magical experience to be on this side with all of us who are here and who experience everything that we experience all the time. The beauty, the love, the joy, the extensive and magnificent experiences are almost unbelievable to those of you who return Home after an extended period upon the Earth.

The concept of not working in order to achieve something or to create something is rather difficult to grasp at first, and it will take a short period of what you conceive of as "time" before you will be able to master everything that we do and everything

The Golden Essence Is YOU

that we master. Know that we are always ready to help you and always ready to guide you, if you just ask. It's always the universal rule: "Ask and you will receive". Though we reiterate this again, and we will continue to tell you, for some of you do have the habit of forgetting many things, and the major part of not getting help for yourself is forgetting to ask, and then not understanding why no one or nothing is helping you. Ask, ask, ask, *always* remember to ask.

We would like to talk now of preparations for achieving the Ascension Vibratory Level.

The vibratory level of planet Earth is rising daily, and those of you who are unaware of this will not be surprised to hear that your lives have become a bit more difficult in the recent past of Earth time, and we point out to you that what we have said before is very necessary for your preparing yourselves to join others whose vibrational levels are already higher than your own.

It is imperative that you joyously aim yourselves in this direction by meditations, affirmations, spending time doing what you call "tuning in" to those of higher vibratory levels such as the Ascended Masters, the Angelic Realm, The Goddess Herself, or what you call The God Itself, what we call The Source Creator of All There Is.

You need to take time every day, to take some minutes of your time, as much as possible, but please do not feel that you need to be excessively devout or that you need to join a religious group of some sort in order to raise your vibrations — it takes only some intent on your part to tune in, to begin to feel yourself a part of a group of beings of a higher vibration than those you spend time with every day.

You need to use the Affirmations we have given you, and we will give you more.

You need to meditate, if this is possible and attractive to you.

Otherwise, you need — you could think of prayer as an avenue for raising your vibrations, simply speaking with that Being that you perceive to be The Creator of All There Is, whether you call that Being "God" or some other name.

We would like for you to know that the name is not important, it is the energy, The Source of Light and Love, the use of love in all facets of your life, the attempts to be loving, kind, gentle, and peaceful toward your fellow travelers upon the Earth is also a valuable resource for you to raise your vibrations, to work with those of lesser accomplishments or those who are in need of physical comfort who are unable to achieve that on their own.

These are all things that you can do to raise your vibrational levels. Anything, which puts you in service, will raise your vibrational levels, anything at all — opening a door for an infirm person, for example, in public somewhere is an act of kindness, which will raise your vibrational level. Everything that you do which is generous, kind, thoughtful, and loving will help you to raise your vibrational level. If you carry that forward into prayer, meditation, repeating of affirmations, and listening to our messages, all of these things will raise your vibrational levels. It need not be what you consider "difficult" for you. It is simply a matter of concentration, intention, and attention upon that which you desire for a dedicated period of time, for example, five minutes occasionally, throughout the day, even one minute as we have suggested before, one minute every hour on the hour to concentrate upon loving thoughts, to concentrate upon us, to concentrate upon the Ascended Masters, to concentrate upon The All There Is—any of this will raise your vibratory level exponentially. If you will take this on every day and remember to accomplish something of these suggestions we are giving you, it will be good for you and good for your path forward in life upon the Earth, and for your life after you have left the Earth.

But, for the Ascension itself, in order to go forward with Gaia, with Mother Earth, in her raising of her vibrations, it is imperative that you raise your vibrations as well, and, as we have indicated, cut the cords of the ties that bind you to others, whether they be cords that they have sent into you, or cords that you have sent into them. It is imperative that you cut these cords as soon as possible so that you will be free of any being holding you back.

You may retain the ties of the heart with those whom you know will be ascending, but we suggest that you cut the ties, even to the heart chakra, of those who will not be ascending. It is up to your discernment, your contact with your Higher Self. When in doubt, cut the cords, all of them, including the heart. If your Higher Self intends for you to have a heart connection with someone, it will re-establish the connection, so be not afraid, if you check with someone with whom you have cut the cords and find there is a new cord connection from heart to heart. In this case, check with your Higher Self to see if the Higher Self has placed this new connection there, and if not, ask the permission, as we have told you, to cut that cord again, if you feel that that person might hold you back in any way.

We know that this information is very confusing to many of you, and we wish you to know that we see you, we see your confusion, we see your pain, we feel your pain, we know what you are experiencing, and we send you our Love and our Energies of Love into your hearts now.

All of you who are listening or who are reading these words, you will now have an infusion of The Energy of Love from The Archangels, from The Angelic Realm, from The Goddess, and from The Creator of All There Is.

If you will just breathe this in now, into your heart, the energy is being sent at this moment, so breathe in — and feel the energy within your hearts — and breathe in again — and feel your heart growing larger with energy — breathe in once more — and when you have taken these three breaths, we suggest that you look into your heart and spread this energy from us throughout your bodies — up into your head, down throughout the rest of your body, and know that when you ASK, you will ALWAYS receive an infusion of Love from us. If you feel alone, call upon us and we will send you Love. If you feel fear, call upon us and we will send you Peace and Love. If you feel <u>any</u> negative emotions, call upon us and we will soothe you until you feel peaceful, free, and loving once more. Know that we are always here to protect you, to heal you, to love you, and to send you our Peace.

And for today, this speaking is finishing.

We wish you to know that we are the Archangels, and many more, and these are our truths for this day upon the Earth.

CHAPTER NINE

ABOUT SOULS AND THEIR RELATIONSHIPS TO HUMANS; CHANGING YOUR CONTRACT WITH YOUR SOUL

As you have expressed interest, we will speak today about the use of crystals to amplify the frequencies of the energies that you receive from us. We would say to begin, that the use of a clear quartz crystal during *"The Meditation of The Journey to the Sea of Love and Light"* will help to amplify the energies that you are receiving from us. When you listen to our words guiding you through the meditation, the use of the crystal will allow you to journey deeper and more clearly to *"The Sea of Love and Light"* of The Creator Source of All There Is.

We would say to those of you who are listening to our voice or reading our words in one format or another, that you should use your intuition or ask your Guides for help, or ask your Higher Self for help, in finding the perfect crystal for you for this meditation. We are also available to guide you in finding the proper crystal for your use, each one of you, and as we have said before, you need only ask for our help and we will give it, most gladly, for we are here to help you in all parts of your life upon planet Earth, no matter what dimension you are in, or what level of achievement, what level of vibratory frequency you have achieved.

It is important for you to know that we trust in you to do that which is best for you, for upon planet Earth, as you know — some of you may *not* know — you have free will, free choice in all matters pertaining to your own personal evolvement, your own personal creativity, and your own personal life.

Where you do NOT have free will is in any attempt to organize the life of another, to interfere with another's free will. It is most important for you to know that the only human being that you have control over is *yourself*. You may think that you have control over another, but that is not the case. The other may *allow* you to take control of them, in a symbiotic relationship where one feeds off the energy of the other and vice-versa, but in truth, it must be an *Agreement*, for, according to universal law, you are not allowed to interfere with any part of another being, as we are not allowed to interfere with any part of your life at any stage, any time, any place.

The Golden Essence Is YOU

The situation is completely changed if you *ask* us for our help. The situation on Earth is changed if you are *asked* by another for your help. You may always offer your services to another, knowing that if they decline, that is their choice for them in that period of time. It is very important that you all understand this "Universal Law of Asking". You may offer, and you may have your offer accepted, but we reiterate, if your offer is declined, that is the end of the story.

Everyone, every soul who imparts its energy into a human, has the sole control over their human, and the human, if it is able to contact the soul, may always ask and ascertain its purpose for existing upon the Earth. Or, if and when you find yourself in another area of the universes, you may always communicate with your Soul in any circumstance.

For many of you upon the Earth, it is almost impossible to contact the soul, for the connection must be clear. The connection must be extremely clear, and most of you — not all, but most of you — enter the Earth with an Agreement with the Soul that you will act independently of the soul's control, and that only in case of dire emergency where it seems that perhaps your existence would end suddenly and you have agreed that the soul may intervene to keep you safe within your body. Only in that case is the soul allowed to arrange events, also suddenly, that will cause a what you call "miracle", in that what seemed to be most definitely leading to your death would suddenly turn into a rescue.

There are situations in which beings upon the Earth decide to end their lives suddenly by stepping in front of a train, for instance. You must know that if this were not the soul's agreement with the being, it would not happen. The human being would in some way be saved, either by someone reaching out to pull them back, or tripping and falling backward; any number of possibilities exist.

But in most cases where you read of what seem to be humans' very sad and unfortunate sudden endings to lifetimes, there is always an "Agreement with The Soul" that the life of the human is to be terminated at that point, and the Soul Part *(that energetic part of a human being)* is to return back to the Soul, via the process of leaving the body behind and coming to this side of the Veil, and doing a Life Review, consulting with counselors on this side and then either deciding, in agreement with the Soul, to return to Earth, or to experiment in some other direction — with existence in some other area. It is almost impossible to describe the process that the Soul Part goes into and through, but we have given you a brief outline of what might be possible.

In order for you to understand more about the perceived disasters, difficulties, or those happenings which occur upon the Earth — the very dramatic bombings, the disasters of suicide bombing, for example, which is happening quite frequently now upon your Earth — in these cases, unless something happens to save the people in the area, you may all know that it is an agreement entered upon on this side of the Veil that all those involved in the bombing, including the bomber, — it is an agreement amongst *all* of them — that this will happen. It is simply a part of experience upon the Earth plane which allows the soul of each of them to broaden its knowledge and its feeling base of possible energetic input which can be transmitted to the Soul

Part when it returns to become human upon the Earth again, or, if needed, when it journeys to another place as another very different type of Being, not human, but alive. These we will not discuss at this point.

As you are all upon the Earth now, and the most important part of your hearing information from us is to learn more about life as a human, and about the disasters and difficult situations, such as the deaths of babies, for example, or the deaths of soldiers. Any sudden, unexplained death is very difficult for you as humans to bear and to understand because of the ways that you have been taught to believe "What Is". If you will look at everything from the perspective we have just shown you, that the soul is gaining experience by whatever it is that the human experiences, you will understand more easily.

We do not say that this will remove your grief at the loss of a loved one who leaves your life suddenly, or even slowly, for the death of the body of a human is perceived to be something quite terrible, when, in fact, as we have already mentioned, it is a, rather like a re-birth, for when you leave the body behind, you come back into the Light, into the Love which permeates everything on this side of the Veil. As we have also said earlier, it permeates everything on *your* side of the Veil as well. You simply do not perceive in the way that we do.

Those of you who have allowed the Veil to be complete are unable to "see" as we see. Those of you who have made a *contract* to have the Veil only partially in place are more easily able to "see" as we see. And there are some of you who come into Earth bodies without that clause in your contract which prevents your "seeing". These you call, — upon the Earth —, you call them "seers", or "psychics". They are able to see energies; they are able to see those elemental beings upon the Earth that most of you cannot see. This includes the fairies, the gnomes, the devas, all of those beautiful energetic beings who "work" on the Earth plane at maintaining the beauty of the plant life, of the mineral life. Yes, they are there. Some of you may *feel* their presences, and some of you may see them, and those of you who, for one reason or another of your Soul and yourself, have the complete Veil in place, — you cannot either see or hear or feel their presences. But know that they are there.

We say to you that if you wish, you may change your Contract at this time. You may all ask your souls, through us, to change your Contract to allow you to see, to allow you to feel, and to allow you to do whatever it is *(that you wish)* with your life upon the Earth from this point forward.

If you wish to change your contract, all you need do is go deeply into meditation, contact us, or contact your Higher Self, state your presence, ask for what it is that you wish — for example, the removal of the Veil —, and promise that you will not abuse the privilege of having the Veil removed. The reason for the Veil is so that you will spend your entire time upon the Earth you have planned for, and you will not leave sooner than that time you have planned to leave. There are some of you who will find it so beautiful when you become aware of everything that is, that you will want to leave the Earth.

We reiterate: You must make the promise that you will stay and fulfill your Contract with your Soul. If you remove the Veil, you

The Golden Essence Is YOU

must still maintain the Contract with your Soul, for it is written that you will abide by your promises. Any promise made to the Soul when you are granted permission to inhabit a human body must be maintained.

Having the Veil removed at some point in your lifetime is optional, so if you reach a high enough vibratory level where you realize your responsibility to your Soul and to yourself as a human, then you may ask to have the clause removed that states you will not "see". You may have the Veil removed. And even then, when you can "see", as we have stated, you must honor your Contract with Your Soul.

We would like to close here for this period of speaking, and ask that you remember always the immensity of the Love that we have for you, the immensity of the Love that your Soul has for you, and the great and magnificent unending Love that The Source of All There Is feels for you. Remember always, you are a Spark of All There Is, The Creator Source, The Universal Light. We ask you to remember always that you are composed of Love and Light.

We are the Archangels and many, many, many more, and these are our truths for this day upon the Earth.

CHAPTER TEN

CHANGE WHAT YOU THINK, FEEL, AND BELIEVE

If you would like, we will speak today about the myriad surprises that one can expect when entering into a deep meditative state, such as the one that you may reach during the journey we have given you, the meditation "*Journey to the Sea of Light and Love*". The deeper you get into this state, the more you can expect of what you might call "visions" of deeper feelings, of phenomena with which you are not acquainted. We do say that it would take, for some of you, a considerable amount of time to reach the deepest level on a regular basis, for you must continue meditating for more than a short period of time in order to achieve the states necessary for the advanced phenomena that you might experience in a deep meditative state. For example, once you have become accustomed to the vibrations and the frequencies of deep meditation, there are always other layers, even deeper, in which your brain waves slow down, bringing you closer to that deep sleep level that you achieve during the night when your bodies are asleep and you are "out" on this side of the Veil, experiencing what you experience here.

We say to you that this course of action—that is, the Ascension Process—takes place over a period of time, so that your Earth body may become accustomed to the changing vibrations.

Most of you are beyond the age of twenty, where you become more immersed in the requirements of civilization: finding a job, working for your sustenance, starting a family, having children, and everything that that entails. But those of you who are older and understand that one can become "mired down" in the requirements of civilization—we do not wish for you to imagine or believe that civilization is a trap.

The third dimensional activities, and attributes of existing in the third dimension, are definitely something that can hold you back from deep meditative states. For one, it is difficult for many to stop *thinking* in order to meditate. The brain loves to be active, the awake brain, and the brain will keep you awake in order to remain active. It loves activity, it loves to think, and in order to meditate deeply, it is necessary to put aside thoughts, and in cases where it is possible for you, to stop your thoughts and to *feel* the vibrations of the brain waves slowing down. It is for this reason that we ask you to *feel* our energies entering into your hearts and to pull those vibrations up into your head before dispersing them downward into the rest of your body.

It is important for the meditative process and also for the healing process that you bring our energies into your heart, move the energies up into your brain — or, as we say, into your head — and then bring the energies in again through the heart and feel them flowing downward into the remainder of the body.

It is quite good to remember this when descending into the deeper states of meditation. Remember that *feeling* of the words as we have given them to you in the meditation of "*The Journey to the Sea of Love and Light*". *Feel* the vibrations rather than listening to the words. The longer, over a period of time, — in this we mean daily —, the longer and more often that you use this meditation, it will become easier for you to *feel* the feelings of the vibrations of the sounds coming from the speaker and from us, through the speaker — it will become easier for you to achieve the deeper meditative states.

When you can *feel* the vibrations, rather than listening to the words, you will have a much deeper experience in *The Sea of Love (The Journey to the Sea of Light and Love)* and you will find that you can more readily achieve healing of your bodies — and by that we mean the physical body as well as all the other bodies which are unseen by most humans, but can be seen by us, of course. The deeper you meditate, the more you *feel* the vibrations, the easier it will be for those parts of your bodies which are not in vibration with our vibrational frequency. They will either change to a more harmonious aspect in your beings, or they will be eliminated.

Any possible manifestations in the etheric of dissonances which might cause dis-ease in the body, if it reaches the physical form, will be ameliorated or eliminated completely by our vibrational frequencies, as translated by you from the voice you are hearing now *(if you are listening to this channeled information.)*

We say to you that for the Ascension Process, it is imperative that you continue meditating. We would suggest that you use our meditation of *Light and Love (The Journey to the Sea of Light and Love)*, but we understand that you may prefer to meditate silently, to yourselves. You might prefer to use a phrase, or what is called a "mantra", that takes you deeper into meditation. We of course allow everything to you, for you have free choice where you are.

We say only that when we transmit our vibrational frequencies to you through this voice *(the co-author's)* or through the paper that you might be reading, or even through the digital format you may have chosen to tune in to, you may receive our vibrations through all of these media, and it is most beneficial for you if you choose to use that way of tuning in to us or to The Source, for in tuning in to us, you are, of course, tuning in to the frequencies of The Source, which we transmit to you through *our* vibrational frequencies.

This may sound confusing to some, but we explain to you that we are in service to The Source of All There Is, to The Creator Light of Love, and we have agreed to be intermediaries, for the energies of The Source are, as you might imagine, words fail us here, but we can say that they are extremely powerful and in need, of necessity, to be, what you call, "stepped down" in frequency, so that the frequency is available to you which is most beneficial.

It is not possible for The Creator's Light to harm you, but for *some* humans — those of you in human form whose vibrational levels are *lower* than those who have been working to raise their vibrational levels — it would be difficult for *you* to receive The Creator's Light *directly from* The Creator, without our altering the frequencies to a more readily accessible level, which is both loving and healing at once. Some of you may feel that this is not necessary, and that is your prerogative. You may of course, address yourselves directly to The Source of All There Is for your healing.

We say to those of you who are in tune with the Angelic Beings of Light who serve The Creator Source of All There Is, that you know our energies to be peaceful, loving, calming, and healing, and we suggest that you choose whatever form it is that you desire for your healing, for you are the creators, in human form, of your lives. You are the creators of your health. You are the creators of your illness. You have free choice, and if you choose to ask us for help in your healing, we are, of course, available to all who ask.

It is necessary always for you to *request* healing assistance from us, and it is always useful for you to understand that *you heal yourselves,* with our help, with the energies we transmit to you of Love, Light, and Healing. We cannot emphasize this enough. It is so important that you understand *you create your illness,* even if you feel it was created by someone else, by some conflict in your life, by some deeply held resentments, by anything that is not a thought of a positive nature.

We urge you to examine your thoughts, to examine your ways of thinking, and to change anything that forms itself into a negative thought into a positive thought. This will take some work on your part, but once you become aware of your thoughts and the ways in which they manifest (and you can hear this in your speech patterns), if you want to be healthy, you need to frame your thoughts in a positive manner, and frame your speech in a positive manner.

Remember always that your body is a conglomerate of cells, each cell of which has a consciousness and is aware of both your speech and your thoughts. Each cell is an independent contractor working inside your body, either for your benefit or for the fulfillment of your negative thinking or negative speaking.

You must know that in this time upon the Earth when all is changing, all is rearranging itself on the physical plane, what is called now the third dimension — some may refer to it as the fourth, or the third/fourth — it matters not — everything that is in this level of human existence and those of you who feel that that is where you are living, you will manifest everything that you think, feel, and speak. It is *imperative* that you understand this, for in order to change anything, you must have a complete understanding of how it works and how it works on Earth for humans in the third dimension, third/fourth dimension, is that *you create your health or your disease.* Of course, you can be influenced by others' attitudes and treatment towards you and of you, but the ultimate journey, and the ultimate *choice* of how you react to others and to your existence upon the Earth is up to you.

The Golden Essence Is YOU

We say again, examine your thoughts, examine your beliefs, examine your feelings, examine most of all your *speaking*, for whatever it is that you speak aloud, it is heard by every cell in your body, and will manifest for you. The closer you come to being in the fifth dimension of the Ascension Process, you *will* begin to see things manifesting more rapidly, and therefore, the negative thoughts, feelings, beliefs, and speaking will happen much more rapidly than you have been accustomed to so far. The third dimension is very slow. It takes quite some time for something to manifest in the third dimension, or third/fourth dimension, but in the fifth dimension, you will begin to see a rapid realization of the effects of any negativity.

And therefore we *urge* you most seriously to begin *now* to change the way you think, the way you feel, your beliefs and the manner in which you speak. This is so important for you. We must stress this over and over:

> BE VERY CAREFUL WHAT YOU **SAY** MOST OF ALL,
> BUT ALSO WHAT YOU THINK, FEEL, AND BELIEVE.
> CHANGE WHAT YOU CAN, NOW, WHILE YOU HAVE TIME.
> CHANGE. CHANGE IS IMPERATIVE.

We would say to you now that we love you with the deepest Love that we can feel, and we send all of you now our most deep feelings of Love. Open your hearts wider to receive the Love that we are sending now. Know that you are loved, that you are honored for your choices, and that we bless you with all of the Light and Love that we could possibly send you now.

We are the Archangels and many, many more, and for this day upon the Earth, the speaking is ended.

CHAPTER ELEVEN

BECOMING A CHANNEL OF LOVE

We would like to speak today of the role of channels — so-called channels — who are messengers for those of us on this side of the Veil, in the Ascension Process.

It is important for everyone to understand that each of you in human form has the capability, innate capability, to hear, see, and feel the information which is available to all and which can be accessed. This process is not easy, but it is attainable by all of you, if you but apply yourselves to clearing a pathway, or the "channel", to the "Other Side", to the higher vibrational frequencies of those of us who reside on this side of the Veil, primarily, and also to those who have returned to this side of the Veil from forays outward, be it upon the Earth, or in other systems. Some of you are also able to open a channel or clear the pathway to those of other planetary systems, what you generally speak of as "Aliens", but who are no more alien to you than you are to God/Goddess/The Creator. They are simply not human in their appearance or their characteristics, in their beingness, wherever it is that they reside. There *are* those who are more humanoid in appearance.

We know this information may be disturbing for some who are hearing this for the first time, but we ask you to listen with your *hearts* and not with your belief systems, for the existence of other life forms in other places *and* even upon the Earth, unseen, is a fact. There are, for example, among you now those who, if you could see them, you would term "fairies"; there are those referred to as "devas", which are similar to fairies. There are what is referred to as "the little people". They are existing in the folklore of all of the more primitive peoples of your planet. They can be known as "the little people", the "menehune" — those terms apply to the smaller elemental beings who care for the basic growths upon the Earth, that is, the plant world, and the mineral world, the animals. These smaller beings care for them and supply them with whatever it is that they need.

However, we say to you today, going back to our original thoughts on this matter, that the messengers, the channels among you, are of two, perhaps three varieties: There are those who decided, before incarnating, to come in with the ability to speak to those of us on this side naturally, as a gift they have given themselves; there are those of you who have given yourself this gift, but veiled it so that you need to clear the

The Golden Essence Is YOU

Veil, or the channel, before being able to speak with us or hear us; and then, there are those of you who do not hear us, but who *sense* us, who *feel* us, who know when we are around, when we are close, and who can receive information through their feeling senses. It is as if they have antennae, feelers, as though they were insects, and they sense all around themselves in all directions, defined information.

The speaker *(the Co-author)* uses this particular ability when driving her car, for example, to sense and feel ahead of her the traffic patterns that are possible. This causes her to be more aware of what is happening upon the road, and this so-called "sixth sense" that she has developed is useful even when she is a passenger in an automobile being driven by someone else, for she has the ability to alert the driver to a possible situation which might be difficult to escape.

In any case, there are those of you who do not trust yourselves or who do not believe it possible that you could become a channel, and so you rely upon those who can. But we reiterate that you *all* have the ability, once you have taken the necessary steps in order to open the passageway, open the "channel" to receive. There are many ways to accomplish this, not the least of which is meditation, in order to open the passageway. Meditation is necessary, patience is necessary, the firm belief that it is possible for you to open in this way, desire, intention, and love are necessary. There are specific steps which must be taken or which are necessary to develop this ability.

Number one is that you must practice daily. Some of you may find it more beneficial to sit quietly at any computer and just type out the thoughts which come to you. Some of you may prefer to take pen and paper and write out what you hear, or what you may be sensing. You need to have a confirmation, and from time to time it may seem hopeless, but we ask you to remain positive, to remember always to avoid negative thoughts about yourself and your ability, and most importantly, avoid speaking aloud any feelings of lack or inability to accomplish the goal which you are aiming for. It is a complex subject, but one which is attainable by all of you.

For the time being, we would say that any pursuits that lead you on a pathway to higher vibrational levels coupled with a desire to create a pathway for the channel is good. Meditating daily and imagining that you are hearing your Guides speaking to you, or your Higher Self, will help a great deal. We ask that you persevere in this, for the time will come when it will be necessary for us to speak to you personally, and you must be able to hear any of us, or your Higher Self, or your Guides.

You must begin to listen more carefully, for it is of the utmost importance that you become more adept at hearing, feeling, sensing, or knowing what it is that you might need to do suddenly. There are many instances upon your planet Earth of the ones who have avoided disaster situations because they had a *feeling* that they should go away from the point where the disaster occurred, shortly before. It is important that all of you understand, for in the future, your relationship with those of us on this side of the Veil will become more and more important, for, as you know, your planet, Gaia, is changing form and vibrations, vibrational frequencies, and there may come a time when you all need to move from where you are, either short-

The Golden Essence Is YOU

term or long-term, and you will be guided, if you will be able to hear, and if you trust us enough to know that we are protecting you when we ask you to move. We may not mean moving from one area to another area, simply moving short distances away from where you might have been. Some of you will be guided to move to other areas of the planet. Some of you will be guided to bring your Light to some of the darker areas. Some of you may suddenly be guided to teach what you know to others. And some of you simply may be asked to stay where you are in order to be of service to those near you.

> WE ASK YOU ALL NOW
> TO BREATHE DEEPLY AND SLOWLY,
> FOR SOME OF YOU
> MAY HAVE BECOME FEARFUL
> HEARING OR READING OUR WORDS
> ON THE SUBJECT OF EARTH CHANGES,
> SO IF YOU WILL JUST NOW
> TAKE A DEEP BREATH – IN – HOLD –
> OUT – IN – OUT – IN – OUT.

We wish to remind you that you are protected at all times, even if it is your choice to return Home during the Earth changes. As we have said, we will welcome you back with open arms, and you may know that you will be celebrated upon your return.

We ask those of you who have, in your Life Plans, decided to remain upon the Earth during the period of the changes, to be prepared to help those in need who may be fearful, — to be of service in any way possible. Be prepared and remain in a loving state, not a fearful state, for fear slows down the vibrations and pushes you backward into a vibratory state which is slower and lower than the one you would have normally without the fear. It is the LOVE vibration that carries you ever higher and higher, the feelings of love, the love for all parts of yourself, and all parts of those close to you, and all parts of those you may not even know.

You have seen, with the outpouring of compassion, love, and relief for the people of Haiti, you have seen how the entire world, all of you, have opened your hearts wider to enfold these people in need, and we say to you the sending of the LOVE vibration to that area has helped them enormously in their struggle, and has allowed them to endure and survive, when without the love, they would have given up. Please remember this at all times, and send love out around this beautiful world that you live in, to all beings, all plants, all animals, all humans, and non-humans alike. Cover everyone and everything in an etheric blanket of warmth and love, and watch the changes unfold.

All of you, together, can help and be of service to this planet and those beings upon it during the Ascension Process by simply *being* Love, and sending vibrations of your love outward in all directions around you. Be aware that the vibration of Love need not go straight forward out of the heart, but indeed is capable of emanating from the heart from all 360 degrees of the circumference of your heart, of your body. We ask you to remember this. There is love in your hands. There is love in your eyes. There is love in your hair. There is love in your skin. Everywhere that *you* are, there is Love.

The Golden Essence Is YOU

If you can open your heart ever wider, there will be more and more love of you to affect those not only near you, but also far away, for every movement that you make creates a wave in the energy body of the Earth, and if every movement you make has the idea, the feeling, the thought, and the qualities of *love* within it, that is what you will send out from you in ever-widening circles, like the pebble in the pond.

Take the time to sit quietly in meditation, and at some point in your meditation, send love out to all. You have no idea how your love can affect others, other beings, even plants, even rocks, even insects who might be annoying you. Send them love and ask them to leave; they most probably will. They come close to you to feel the love, and if you send it ahead, they perhaps will not come too close, if you do not wish it. Those of you, who *do* wish it, send the love with an invitation: *(whispered)* "Come here — Come here". All creatures sense the welcoming vibrations or the unwelcoming vibrations, and you know this to be true. You have seen those beings who fear snakes, for example, or spiders, and their fear attracts those beings to them and reinforces the fear. If they would only breathe deeply, become calm, and emanate the vibrations of Love, not only would they alleviate their fears, but they would see that the animals or insects would honor the unspoken request *(whispered)* "Go away".

You may have heard it said that snakes "know heart". We assure you that snakes *do* know your innermost feelings in your heart, and whether or not you are accepting and loving towards them, or fearful and destroying. They are totally aware of the vibrational frequencies of Love and of Fear, and all that implies.

Marilyn Zschau Baars

We say to you that in order to become a channel or a messenger of Love, it is good to concentrate upon this, to meditate upon this, and to dedicate yourselves to becoming beings of Light and Love.

We are the Archangels, and many, many more. We send you now a blanket of Love to cover you and bring you peace this day upon the Earth.

And these are our truths.

CHAPTER TWELVE

THE IMPORTANCE OF "NOW" TIME

We would like to discuss today the seriousness of progressing along a path that carries you back toward your true essence, which is that of a Being of Light and Love. We say also that this pathway can be difficult for some, if not for all of you who are hearing or reading these words, and we say to you that the rewards are great, for the Earth is changing quite rapidly, and those of you who are working diligently to raise your vibratory frequencies will be rewarded with the most beautiful experiences that a Being of Light and Love can experience in human form. It is not exactly the same as being here on this side of the Veil, but you will come very, very close to feeling the same way that you feel here, and those feelings of freedom, of lightness, of love, of capability, of intention, of attention — those feelings will help you all to attain and maintain your places in the fifth dimension of Creativity, of Love, and of Light Eternal.

Some of you reading these words, or hearing them spoken, may have a feeling of disbelief, but we assure you that we speak only the truth, and we assure you also that if you join everyone who is already treading upon this path towards Light and Love, Acceptance and Peace, if you join everyone else, you will *all* reach the fifth dimension and beyond, depending upon your intentions and what it is that you desire to achieve in this particular lifetime upon planet Earth.

We assure you once again, that the goal is attainable and that you will make it, *if* you apply yourselves, meditate daily, use affirmations which are positive and uplifting, work to transform your negative beliefs, any negative feelings, into positivity and into Light. See that which you wish to become. See yourself as that Being of Love and Light *now* in "present time", for in the fifth dimension and beyond, there is no "Past", there is no "Future" — there is only "NOW".

In order for you to become accomplished at understanding this concept of NOW TIME, it is very important for you to begin practicing NOW TIME *now,* in the "present" upon the Earth. If and when you catch yourselves projecting forward into what you call "the future", bring yourselves gently back to the NOW and experience fully whatever it is that you are doing NOW. If you find yourselves regressing backward into what seem to be previous events upon the Earth in this current lifetime, gently bring yourself back to the present time, NOW TIME, and experience everything that you are experiencing in NOW TIME, even if it is only to become aware that you are breathing in and out.

If you are sitting quietly in meditation, and your mind begins to lapse into its habit patterns of wandering, gently remind yourself that you are experiencing only NOW TIME, and gradually you will establish a pattern — or a habit, as some of you like to call it —, a pattern of oneness with yourself, with us, with all of the Beings of the Light, and with The Creator Source Itself. Keep reminding yourself that you only wish to experience NOW TIME, that in NOW TIME you may make a list of what you wish to happen, but, as best you can, remain aware of NOW rather than the "future".

Say, for example, that you need to shop for food. Sit down in NOW TIME with a piece of paper and pen or pencil and ask yourself, "What is it that I need NOW?" And whatever comes to mind, you write that down. You ask again, "What else do I need NOW?" and so forth. In this way, when you make your list, you will not project yourselves forward, for example, into your car, or into the store, or into the process of choosing within the store; but you will remain in the NOW by simply asking yourself, "What is it that I need NOW?" This will be a good exercise for many of you and something quite different from the way in which you have been accustomed to making lists of what you might need in what you have perceived as your "future", but we tell you once again, the "future" is NOW, the "past" is NOW: All is NOW TIME. Once it is gone, it is gone, and that which has not yet happened is within your "present", NOW.

Marilyn Zschau Baars

In order to create, you need to remain in the NOW. See what it is that you wish to have or that you wish to become, and believe us when we tell you it will happen much more rapidly than you can possibly imagine. Remember that NOW TIME is extremely powerful, that wishes and desires that you express in NOW TIME will be created sooner than you think.

The word of caution here: You must become accustomed to creating only *positive* thoughts, for as we have said, once you are fully within the fifth dimension and beyond, everything that you *think* will manifest INSTANTLY. At least now, upon the Earth, you have some extra — what you call "time". You have extra "time" in order for that which you desire to manifest. If you find yourselves thinking negative thoughts about something or someone, you still have some "time", before it manifests, to remove the negative thought and to replace it with a positive thought.

You may also erase negative thoughts and wishes by using terminology that will cause the negative event to evaporate. You have the free will to choose whatever terms might be necessary for you to utter in order to cancel out a negative expression, or a negative thought. We leave that up to you. Some have learned the expression "Cancel, cancel", which is good. You may also simply express verbally aloud, "I wish to remove this negative thought from my existence. I wish to replace it with this positive thought", and then you imagine whatever it is that you wish to say instead of the negative thought. Negative pictures you may place an "X" upon and replace them with positive pictures. This is an area that we leave completely up to you, for it is your right to create for yourselves whatever it is that you wish to create.

The Golden Essence Is YOU

If you are in the habit of thinking negative thoughts or seeing negative pictures, we urge you now to change this manner of behavior as soon as you possibly can, for this is a habit pattern which you do not wish to take with you when you ascend to the fifth dimension and beyond.

YOU MUST BE THE MASTER OF YOUR MIND.

YOU MUST BE THE MASTERS OF YOUR MINDS, ALL OF YOU.

Those of you who have come to this material not understanding anything of which we speak, we urge you most gently to become aware of that which we are telling you now, and to change as much as you possibly can, quickly, quickly, for the time is advancing, the "future" is *now*, the "past" is no longer interesting to you. What is interesting is "NOW", *now*. You must exist *now* in the "NOW". It is most important. We cannot urge you more strongly than to say, "Change these habits *now*".

We would like also to say, to those of you who *are* already aware of the importance of NOW TIME, that some of you may also have ingrained, buried beliefs that need to be excavated, brought to the light, examined, and changed. Your negative beliefs may be deeply, deeply hidden within your psyche, and we say to you, it is *most* important that you find a way for yourselves to bring these beliefs up to the forefront of your minds to examine them, to find a way to change them, and to do this also as quickly as possible. These changes are SO important for your advancement to the fifth dimension and beyond. We cannot emphasize this strongly enough. Please, *please* heed our words, and do this work now, *now*, NOW.

In addition to this, we would encourage you to understand the importance of everything that you think, everything that you say, everything that you do, everything that you feel, and everything that you know. Sometimes there are those of you who feel that you *know* everything that you need to know, but until you have changed *all* in your being that is of a negative nature, in truth, you do not know everything. Become humble. Become open. Become willing to hear what you need to hear. Become able to change. Become aware of what is required for changing. It is *so* important, SO important.

We ask you now to take time every day, in the *now*, to meditate in one form or another. If you are not able to sit quietly and close your eyes to concentrate upon the Light and the Love that you all desire, then choose an affirmation (or two or three) to use for one particular day, and repeat that aloud for yourselves whenever possible. You need not disturb other people with your speaking aloud. You know there are always places you can find which are private. You can always find a place where you can speak aloud without fear of disturbing someone else. It is not very difficult to achieve this.

Do whatever it is that you need to do in order to change those beliefs that no longer serve you, those negative thoughts that no longer serve you. Change as much as you can, sooner rather than later. And always be aware that you are constantly creating with your thoughts, with your words, with your mind, with your feelings.

The Golden Essence Is YOU

Endeavor to keep an even keel. And ever endeavor to find your center of balance. Endeavor to remain upright, friendly, peaceful, loving, kind, capable, deserving.

Allow yourselves to love yourselves, for in loving yourself, you love all others, and you love The Source, who created you.

And for this day on Earth, this speaking is ended.

CHAPTER THIRTEEN

THE ASPECTS OF LOVE; ALIENS AMONG US

We would like to speak today of love in all its forms, be it the love of mother for the child, husband for the wife, the child for the parents — all of the aspects of Love that you could possibly imagine, and we would like to say to begin, that even though we have told you that Love Is All There Is, we have also told you that these words sound simple, but they are not.

For many of you it is difficult to comprehend "All There Is", and indeed, this is a concept that can be very confusing for many humans. There is also, on the part of your egos, a tendency to couple thoughts that go in this direction with the emotional feeling of FEAR. This prevents you from going deeper into the visualizing of All There Is, for indeed, the thoughts of what is beyond this universe lead to the thoughts around Eternity, and then the ego steps in and creates the fear-based picture of destruction of All There Is, which is not possible. The ego does this in order to protect you and to protect your brain from becoming so involved in frightening pictures that could, over time, create such a large problem for the brain that it might consider shutting down and not seeing anything any longer. It could also lead some humans who might be already mentally unstable to become so much more so that they would not be able to return to the concept and place of what you all have agreed to call "REALITY" here upon The Earth.

And so, perhaps it would be good for us now to explain a bit more about "All There Is", in terms which you can all understand, in pictures which are non-threatening, and in feelings which are those positive feelings that you all enjoy feeling — the feelings of being protected, the feelings of comfort, the feelings of deep love, and the feelings of things remaining as they are. We wish to talk with you about these things, specifically because the Earth is going through some major changes now, and in the upcoming periods of Earth time.

You have already seen that volcanic activity is increasing upon the Earth. You have seen that earthquake activity is increasing. You have seen that the winds are becoming more powerful, and also that rain is falling all over the globe, even in places where there is not usually precipitation of rain. These are all the results of the Mother, Earth, who some prefer to call Gaia — these are all signs that she is ascending. She is going through a cleansing process, as are those of you who are aware that a cleansing process is required and that a cleansing process is beneficial for your earthly form at this time, in order for you to ascend along with Gaia, Mother Earth. You have heard talk, perhaps, about the third dimension, the fourth dimension, and the fifth dimension and beyond. Those of you who have not heard about this will hear it now.

The Earth is moving toward the state of unconditional love, which can be found now only in the higher dimensional levels, above the level that you call five, the fifth dimension. You have heard it said, perhaps, that the third dimension, and including the fourth- dimensional aspect of time, is a place of conditionality, and where conditions exist in the sense of love — speaking of love — being unconditional. True unconditional love is not possible in the third dimension. It may be possible for unconditional love to manifest in what *seems* to be the third dimension, through an advanced Being of Light who exists physically upon the Earth, but whose energy field, and whose mind, and whose etheric body are existing in the fifth dimension, and they are bringing forth, these esteemed Beings of Light in human form, they are bringing forth what seems to be unconditional love in the third dimension. But we say to you that this process that they are in is an illusion for those of you in the third dimension, firmly in the third dimension, and that they can transform their feelings of love for you and for all things upon this planet. They can transform their feelings from the highest form of unconditional love into what is perceived by the rest of you as "unconditional love", and an explanation of the process we believe is not necessary.

Suffice it to say, that for most of you, true higher vibrational Love — what is considered unconditional love — is not possible, even when you *think* that you are emanating unconditional love. Unless you are of an extremely high vibratory frequency, you will be emitting love with conditions. You will not truly be able to demonstrate unconditional love upon the Earth until after the Earth has ascended to the fifth dimension and you, along with her, and you all are living in what some might term "Utopia", the place of unconditional love, the place which is closer to The Source of All There Is and Its Love for you and all of Its creations.

Multifunctionality for the dimensions beyond the third/fourth is, in general — and we can only speak in generalities here — incomprehensible to most of you. Those of you who have visions and who travel consciously out of the body, and whose vibrational frequencies are of an extremely high level, may journey forward, upward, around and about, below and beyond, and into so-called higher levels. But we would actually ask you to consider that they are simply "other" levels, "other" places, with a higher vibrational frequency than that of the Earth at this moment, in this time, in the year 2010.

Many of you wish to know the significance of 2012, and we say to you that we have asked you to remain in NOW TIME. If you remain in NOW TIME, all will be revealed in NOW TIME. Take care that you do not allow your egos to create negative scenarios that may be very frightening for you. There are many such opportunities to join with the masses in creating a so-called "future" in the year 2012, in which many disasters will befall the Earth, and will create the end of humankind, as you know it today.

The Golden Essence Is YOU

WE ASSURE YOU THAT THIS WILL **NOT** HAPPEN.

There will be changes to the Earth, and there will be the opportunity for all of you to choose your own particular existences and how you wish to live upon the Earth, and you may choose which Earth you wish to live upon, the one still in 3-D/4-D, or the emerging new Earth of 5-D and beyond. Believe us when we say there will be NO enormous cataclysmic event that will destroy Earth at this time. It is not the future or the NOW TIME of the Earth to destroy herself completely.

There are enough of you who have answered the call to "Wake Up", to become aware of "What Is". In truth, the reality of your existence upon the Earth and all possible futures for you is in NOW TIME, so remember, it is your choice to ascend *with* the Earth, and we have spoken of some of the ways in which to raise your vibrational frequency, for the raising of the vibrational frequency is the one actual, truly *necessary* factor involved in ascending. There are many other things that can be accomplished, but the major factor revolves around your vibrational frequency and whether it is what is called "high enough" or we would say, "*fast* enough". Your vibrational frequency must become faster in order to exist in the higher and faster vibrational frequencies of the fifth dimension and beyond.

The difference between life on Earth and life elsewhere in your universe is the difference between *your* vibrational frequencies in 3-D/4-D and *their* vibrational frequencies, which may be very much higher, and yes, for those of you curious about this, those

101

beings from other planetary systems, other frequency systems, other light systems, those beings, if they should be able to slow their vibrations enough so that they could come onto the Earth and meet with you, (they) would need to slow their vibrations down extensively in order for you to be able to *physically* see them. There are some among you now who are not visible, for they are vibrating too rapidly. Some of you may sense that they are near. Some of you who have higher vibrational levels may be able to see them sporadically, and many of you can see them when you are out of your body or in a deep sleep state during your night.

They are not here to harm you; they are here to observe. They are here upon the Earth to learn from *you*, not you from them. They are not here to save you. They are not here to teach you. They are allowed simply *only* to observe. You need not fear them. You need not believe the fear-makers in the moving-picture industry, or the fear-makers in your television industry, or in your news media industry. These, as most of you are most probably aware, are elements that are interested in capturing you for monetary advantage, that is all. We are scanning now . . . and we do not see at this point that any of them have any ulterior motives to actually frighten you out of your wits, as is sometimes verbalized. They are creating products for you to view; they are creating them for those of you who enjoy being frightened, nothing more, and of course, they do not understand the true meaning of what the Ascension Process is.

We will now take our leave of you for this day, and we tell you in truth we are those Beings of Light you call the Archangels, and we are, as you are, all creations from The Source of All There

The Golden Essence Is YOU

Is. We are filled with Love for you, and admiration that you have all come to Earth at this time in its history to experience the Ascension. You are ALL deeply admired on this side of the Veil, and even beyond.

All of the universes are aware of what is happening here, and all, *all* applaud you for your courage, your love, and your generosity. Because you are here upon the Earth, we are honored to be able to serve you by sending you our Love, our Unconditional Love, flowing it forth to you at all times. All you need do is open your hearts and receive it.

We are the Archangels and many, many more, and these are our truths this day upon the Earth.

CHAPTER FOURTEEN

LIFTING THE VEIL FROM YOUR EYES; THE LIGHT WITHIN; WAKE UP!

We would like to speak with you today about the length of time necessary for this book to be finished, since it is a subject that you have recently spoken about. We see this book as not the usual length that you would expect of a book of speakings from Beings beyond the Veil. It is to be a celebration and an acknowledgement of the dissemination of information to those of you upon planet Earth, who are curious about the Ascension Process, who are curious about the year 2012, who are curious about the Mayan Prophecies, the Hopi Prophecies, and who are perhaps expecting the Earth to end as you know it. This will not be the case. We assure you that the world will not end, the Earth will not stop spinning, there will be no asteroid destruction of the Earth. There will be no alien destruction of the Earth.

The only destruction of the Earth that is allowed to happen is that created *by humans* in their disregard for the beautiful gift that you have been given in this planet. The removal of giant trees, the pollution of the oceans, the pollution of the air that you breathe — these are the sorts of things that are being created by those of you upon planet Earth who are not aware of the necessity that your bodies have for clean air, clean water, and oxygen, which is created by the giant trees. The rainforests of your planet are most necessary for the continuation of life as you know it upon this planet, but as we have often said, we do not interfere. You are allowed to do as you please, and the consequences may not please you, the results may not please you. The Earth is a living, sentient being. She is well aware of the dangers to all life upon the planet at this time, and therefore, she is ascending to a higher vibrational level than is currently maintained upon the Earth in the third dimension (3D/4D).

The vibratory level upon the Earth has been rising steadily over the past years and many of you are well aware of this, and some of you, not at all. We have already spoken of the physical changes that you are beginning to see occurring more and more rapidly now. These are the manifestations of the Earth becoming more a Being of Light during the Ascension Process.

The Golden Essence Is YOU

Those of you who have created the third-dimensional/fourth-dimensional Earth as it is today will either remain upon the Earth as it is today, with the consequences of your creations, or, if you begin to see the Light, you will begin your own Ascension Process, if that is possible, for, as we have said, you *must* raise your vibratory level. Your vibratory frequencies must be faster, higher, more light-filled. You must become more like *us* on what you call the "Other Side of the Veil", in order for you to exist in the vibratory frequencies of the New Earth. You will *not* be able to live upon the New Earth if you think that you can bring your old patterns with you. This is not possible. They must either fall away, and you must change, or you must remain behind.

The beauty, purity, and light of Gaia is already shining once more, as in "The Beginning", and those of you who are vibrating fast enough are able to see this already occurring. You will notice that the colors become more vibrant, that the sky and the clouds (*become*) more beautiful, that the sunlight is more than you have ever experienced in this lifetime. It is happening *now*. The rains are cleansing, the air is cleansing, the Earth herself is growing, and all of the creatures upon the Earth are doing their chosen tasks of creating the New Earth as she once was: youthful, beautiful, with clear air, clean water, and beings living upon her whose only desire is to live in peace and love.

There will be no more war. There will be no more negativity. There will be newness. And there will be understanding of the place of humans within the cosmos. Many changes are coming, and we urge you to begin *now*. *Now* is the time for the beginning again. Envision your beautiful planet Earth in all of her original purity, beauty, love, light, peace, magnificence, and all of the beings upon her living in harmony, peacefully coexisting, loving one another, caring for one another, caring for the Earth.

We ask you now to go forth also this day with the vision thoroughly placed in the forefront of your minds of yourselves as gigantic Beings of Light and Love, spreading the Light and Love before you and around you wherever you go, bringing peace, love, and beauty wherever you are, treating all humans with respect and patience, for there are many who are feeling the great pressure to change and who are unwilling or unable to answer the call. These will remain behind, and you will be challenged to interact with them because they will become more and more difficult to interact with. You may already have experienced the natural frustration of interacting with a human being of great negativity. Before the Ascension Process is final, you will need to remember that these beings do not know what you know, that they are struggling in their lives, that they are frustrated. They are aware that something is changing, but they do not know what it is.

The desire — our greatest desire — is that those of you who come upon these words, whether spoken, or seen, written down, — it is our greatest desire that you hear the message, that the veil falls away from your eyes, and that you are able to comprehend the message that we are sending forth to you.

Wake up *(whispered)*, wake up *(whispered)*, WAKE UP, and know the truth of who you truly are, for you are Great Beings of Light encased in darkness and negativity, and we desire to be able to offer you our services, to help the veil disappear from your eyes, to help you to **see** again the beauty of your true existence, the Light that is covered, the Love that is hidden, but we need for you to *ask* us to serve you. We are not allowed to interfere, but oh, we wish most ardently, we wish to be of service in the times ahead when it will not be easy for you to remain upon this planet in the darkness.

Join us in the Light, come with us into Love, celebrate with us the unconditional love of the fifth dimension and beyond. We invite you to join with all of your fellow travelers who *are* awake, who *are* aware, and who *know* who they truly are, and they know their place in the universe, and they know you, and they call to you along with us, "WAKE UP, WAKE UP NOW, WAKE UP, and celebrate yourselves, WAKE UP, and join with us in the Ascension process. WAKE UP and come with us to the most beautiful places, the most beautiful Light, join with the most beautiful Beings of Light and Love".

Be not afraid, for fear is a vibration that slows you down and holds you back. Be courageous. Take the steps necessary to begin to understand what truly *is* the Truth of the universe, the Truth of your creation, the Truth of your existence. Become aware of the importance of *you*. You are brilliant Beings of Love and Light. You are here upon the Earth as spirit in flesh, and to spirit you will return, one day. And for now, know that you are Eternal Beings of Light. You NEVER die. Death does not exist beyond the Veil. Life is Eternal. The Creator is Eternal. YOU ARE ETERNAL BEINGS OF LIGHT, BEINGS OF LOVE. And we love you *so* very much, that we want you *all* to ascend.

It is our hope that those of you who discover these words, whether written or spoken, will be able to *feel* the truth, and will open your eyes to the truth of the meaning of your existence, and will know once again that magnificent feeling of unconditional love, which exists very high now. We ask you to pass the word along, those of you who are already awake and those of you who are awakening. Be not afraid! Drop a small hint, leave this book lying around for others to find, help in any way that you can, help the others to awaken. Tell them who they are, see them for yourselves as Beings of Light. The Light will be hidden, it may be difficult to see, but if you look hard enough, you may be able to see a glimmer, the beginnings of a flickering of the Eternal Flame of Love that glows within each heart of *all* of you in human form, even those that you would judge to be evil.

We ask you to attempt to see beyond the actions of certain humans that may seem to be "wrong" in your judgment. See beyond the negativity of their existences, see the Light flickering within. It may be only a small flame, very small, but it is a flame that cannot be extinguished by any actions of a negative nature. Know that every one of you upon this planet has set goals for yourselves and your souls, and there are those of you who are learning about extreme negativity. If they are known to you, please feel free to send them Love. Please feel free to send them Love. They will either accept it, or reject it, but you will know the truth, and you will have *your* experience of generosity to add to your soul's "Library of Experiences".

Know that we love you without measure, that we know how difficult it is for many to live upon planet Earth. We are here to serve you. You need only ask.

The Golden Essence Is YOU

We are the Archangels this day, many, many, many, and we flow forth our Love to you now. Open your hearts even wider to receive the Love that we send. We enfold you in our wings of Light, and for this day, these are our truths, and the speaking is ended.

CHAPTER FIFTEEN

THINKING WITH THE HEART

TO THE CO-CREATORS:

We would like to speak today of the importance of your role in the disseminating of this information which we bring to you — and by "your" we mean both of you. Regarding these challenges you are currently having with being able to present our information to the, what you call "the outside world", the public, know that once you start, nothing can stop you from being able to disseminate the information we are bringing through to you, for you, and for others. We ask you to persevere in all cases, finding ways to bring our messages out and onto the Earth.

Marilyn Zschau Baars

You are the only ones currently writing a book with information from us and from The Source Of All There Is. Many will be surprised to hear that we are bringing through information from The Creator, but since we are all ONE, and we all come from The Creator, we do not see anything unusual in this.

The human race likes to place information in organized files, so that they can return to see it again. But we say to you that organizing files is not the best way to receive our information, but to *listen with your hearts,* to open your hearts wider when you become aware that we are speaking directly to you. Open your hearts wider, and *feel* the vibrations of the tones, of the consonants, of the vowels, *feel* the words as they come through your auditory senses and into your brain, and you hear them as you *(the Co-author)* speak, and those of you listening to this speaking hear it as our messenger *(the Co-author)* speaks to you, so open your hearts to *feel* the words.

It is much better for you to *feel* the vibrations of what we are transmitting to you, rather than simply listening with your ears, which takes the information into a different part of the body, into the brain, and the brain has the ability to *forget* what it has heard. *The heart does not forget.* The heart remembers everything that comes to it, through it, and stays within it. It is almost as if the brain is a separate entity, and the heart is a second brain, but the brain of the heart is a *feeling* brain, and the brain in your head is a thinking, calculating instrument.

The heart is the most important organ in your body, for without your heart, you would be here with us. But if you would not be on the Earth plane, breathing, living, feeling, sensing, thinking, — no, no, your body would cease to exist without the heart, and you would leave it behind and come Home. And so it is, that we point out once again, that the heart is the most important organ in the body.

The heart is the center of your deepest feelings. Oh, we know that your emotional center is your third chakra, but we say to you the emotions that reside in the third chakra are not the same as the emotions of the *heart*. The emotions of the heart are all of a positive nature, whereas those emotions in the solar plexus chakra can be more of a negative nature, although the positive emotions may also be felt there. It is not that you do not feel positive emotions in the third chakra, but that *you do not feel negative emotions in the heart*. That is the important difference.

It is the *heart* that responds to *Love*. It is the *heart* that emanates *Love*. It is the *heart* that *heals*. It is the *heart* that *sustains you*. It is the pulsing of the heart that maintains your body. Oh, we know that you need the brain for the impetus and you need the great healing ability of the brain for that nitty-gritty business of taking care of details, but in truth, in the final analysis, if you truly wish to be healed of anything, you need to go through the heart, for without the heart, the brain is a cold, calculating computer.

IT IS THE HEART THAT CAUSES TRUE HEALING.

IT IS THE HEART THAT LOVES.

You can choose to use either the third chakra or the fourth chakra in reference to yourself. You can choose to use the third chakra with the positive *and* the negative to feed your brain feelings which create negative thoughts about yourself, but if you go through the heart to send the brain the impulses to love yourself, that is the path to healing. The love of self sent from the heart to the brain and from there throughout the entire body to every cell — it is the *heart* that speaks to the cells 'n *Love*.

So anytime you feel that you need a healing, look to your feelings and your thoughts about yourself. Look to see if you have been feeding yourself negative impulses about yourself, or if you have been feeling positive feelings of love for yourself. We know that this may seem confusing to some of you, but we assure you that if you spend time alone with yourself, telling yourself in feelings that you're okay, that you're doing well, that you're doing the best that you can do, we assure you this is the best way to become healthy, if you are not, or to remain healthy, if you are.

As we have said before, every cell in your body has a consciousness all its own, and hears and feels everything that you say and feel. Be very, very careful how you express yourself with thoughts or feelings about yourself. Dispense with negative thoughts. Dispense with negative feelings about yourself, for if you feel negative feelings about yourself, you can well imagine what you are feeling about others. When you truly love yourself and you tell yourself that, you will then be able to love others — not before.

And so we would recommend that you take time every day to feed yourself not only food, which sustains your body, but also thoughts and emotions of a positive nature which heal

The Golden Essence Is YOU

you, which heal your psyche, and which ultimately heal your body.

Many people do not like the responsibility of caring for themselves. They want someone else to do it. They are stuck in the feelings of childhood, when Mother and Father took care of them. You must, you *must* come out and away from those feelings of needing to be taken care of. Oh, there are usually people willing to take care of you, but we tell you that they will not take as good care of you as *you* take care of *you*, for you are the only one who is living inside your body, and you are the only one who knows what you really need. No one else can anticipate what you need.

Let us make a correction here: To state that no one else can anticipate what you need, applies only to the Earth plane, for your Guides are always aware of you and your needs, your Higher Self is always aware of you and your needs, WE are aware of you and your needs. But no one else is allowed to interfere in your life. You are the only one in charge. You are the boss of your body, and you need to take control now if you have not already done so. You need to feed yourself the right foods for the optimum functioning of your physical self, and they *(your cells)* will tell you when they are not receiving what they need. You need to take charge of your exercise, of the fresh air that you get, of the sunshine, of all those things that you know are necessary for good health. YOU are in charge. YOU are the boss of your body.

Write yourself a little note and stick it up on your mirror to remind you:

Marilyn Zschau Baars

I AM THE BOSS OF MY BODY.

I AM THE HEAD OF THE CORPORATION OF CELLS.

I ASK MY CELLS TO COMMUNICATE WITH ME.

I ASK MY CELLS TO LET ME KNOW WHAT THEY NEED.

All of these things you can do from time to time as a checkpoint, and they will tell you — believe us when we say they will tell you — what they need, IF you ASK. It is the law of the universe. You must *ask* in order to *receive*. Ask and you shall receive.

Some have said that you must ask "if it is for my highest good", and we tell you that is a good phrase, but need not be asked every time, need not be stated every time. We *know* what is in your heart, and we know that when you ask for something, you intend it for your highest good. We know this. Your Guides know this. Every part of you knows this. If you state it once in your life, that is enough.

And so we say to you: Take care of these bodies that you have. Work with them diligently to bring their vibrational level higher and faster. Bring in more light, bring in more love, bring in more beauty, bring in more happiness, bring in everything that feeds you, physically, emotionally, mentally, and spiritually. Take the time to meditate for your spirit. Take the time to eat good food for your body. Take the time to think healthy thoughts, and most of all, take the time to *love* and be loved. Allow yourselves the possibility of feeling more *love* and feeling more loving in you-life.

The Golden Essence Is YOU

Love yourselves as we love you, if you can imagine what that must be like, for here where we are, we live in Unconditional Love. We love you unconditionally. You need not do something to be loved by us. Because you *are*, because you exist, because you come from The Source, the Light of The Source shines in each and every one of you. It is your origin and The Source Is LOVE.

If you could see your LIGHT, you would have an overwhelming feeling of the deepest love for yourself, for you shine so brightly. Each one of you is a small part of The Creator, and we say "small" only because we know the immensity, the magnificence, the greatness, the hugeness of Source, of All There Is. It is indescribable. The Source of All There Is is indescribably beautiful. There are no words to speak of the beauty, the glory, the gloriousness, the magnificence, the grandiosity — none of these words in *your* language are capable of describing THE ONE, THE GREATEST LOVE that exists. Know that you are only "small" in relation to the largeness of The Creator.

So remember that you are The Creator in human form, sent here to Earth to expand the knowledge of The Source. Every experience that *you* have, The Source has. Know that every thing that you do, that you say, that you feel, is done, said, and felt by The Source of All There Is. Perhaps if you can remember this in your interactions with others, you might choose to speak, to feel, to act, in a different way.

And so we say to you today that we love you endlessly, no matter what. It does not matter to us that you may think yourselves "bad". It matters not to us that you may think yourselves "better" than others. It matters not to us what you think about yourselves, about others. What is important is that you *feel* Love and if you do not *feel* Love, that you choose to find a way to begin *now* to *feel* Love at all times, in all places, and that you choose to begin thinking with your heart, instead of with that third chakra or with your brain.

Allow yourselves to grow, just a bit, every day. Fill yourselves with light, just a bit, every day. And begin again to become that Great Being of Light that you *are* on this side of the Veil. Become a Great Being of Light in human form. And begin your service to All There Is and to others traveling along with you on Planet Earth.

We are always here to help you. You need only ask.

We are the Archangels and many, many more, and for this day, the speaking is ended.

CHAPTER SIXTEEN

THE FIELD OF GOLDEN ESSENCE: A FIFTH DIMENSIONAL VISUALIZATION

We would like to say today to all of you that the path to the fifth dimension and through the Ascension Process is filled with obstacles that you must overcome in order to reach the state of a higher vibration of your physical body and all of your other bodies, from the etheric outward. We urge you to remember to remain in NOW TIME and to keep your attention upon the goal, so to speak, of achieving fifth-dimensional vibratory status for *all* of your bodies, not just the physical. Anything that you can do in order to speed up your vibrations will help you along this path and will ease the obstacles to the side.

Some of the things that you need to be aware of, or to watch for, are contained within your belief systems. Do everything you can, as we have suggested, to find all of your negative beliefs, those beliefs that might hold you back, and clear them using whatever method you prefer. Make sure that you have begun the process of cord-cutting, and that you continue this until you have cut every cord that you can possibly conceive of. And remember to call upon us, or your Guides, or your Higher Self for assistance with this, for it is most important that you cut these cords before very long.

You need to become aware that the Earth is experiencing changes in her physical body as well, and remain secure in the knowledge that you are safe. Even if you have a contract to return Home during this next period of Earth years, please remember: being on this side of the Veil is not a punishment — it is a source of unending joy and happiness. So rest assured that you are always safe, even if you decide to leave your body behind.

Your physical body is not eternal, but *you* yourself, your energies, your etheric body, your mental body, your emotional body, your spiritual self — all of you together are part of a great, a great and enormous body of Light called a "Soul" by you. Altogether, in all of your knowingness, in all of your energy, you are a grandiose Being of Light filled with Love and a very high energy. Remember always that you are a creation directly from The Source Light, The All There Is, and you are, therefore, All There Is, existing now in human form upon the Earth. But eventually, you will all be back Home here on this side of the Veil, in your Light Bodies, going about your business, learning, teaching; whatever it is that you choose to do, you may do that here — helping humans, guiding humans, guiding others elsewhere in the universe, creating worlds — all is available to you on this side of the Veil.

So remember that Mother Earth is changing, and that there *does* exist the possibility that you may have decided to return Home. Do not allow your egos to frighten you with negative pictures. Keep foremost in the front of your mind your True Essence, the knowledge of who you truly are: *A Great Being of Light and Love.* When you can maintain this vision of yourself in your brain at all times, you will raise your vibratory level exponentially, and you will begin to take on the traits that you wish to have: generosity, kindness, love, respect, honoring —, all of the positive qualities, or attributes.

✿✿✿

VISUALIZATION: THE FIELD OF GOLDEN ESSENCE

We ask you now to close your eyes for a few moments, and to imagine and see in your mind's eye fields of Golden Essence, and imagine yourself walking forward, or flying, if you prefer, into this Field of Golden Essence. It is as if you are standing upon the Earth in a great, endless field of wheat, very large-growing wheat, waving gently in the breeze, but where we are asking you to walk, or float, is in a Field, similar to the wheat, of Golden Light and Essence of Love, with the sweetest perfume, and everywhere you move, the fragrance becomes something new and more wonderful, and as you move through and around and within The Golden Essence, you feel within your hearts the most beautiful feelings of peace, of unending Love, and beauty, — beauty that you have not known upon the Earth, for this is a part of Home, this Field of Golden Essence, and within and around this Field are trees whose leaves move with the breeze, and who emanate their own perfumes, that mix with the perfumes of The Golden Essence and they give off a tinkling sound of bells much more beautiful than the sound of any bell you have ever heard, and you are in awe of the beauty that you see and sense all around you, and you feel *light*, lighter than a feather, lighter than air, lighter than sunlight, and you are transported and lifted simply by your thoughts. If you wish to float, you float. If you wish to fly, you fly. If you wish to simply *be* in the center of The Field of Golden Essence, you are. If you wish to become *one* with The Field of Golden Essence, you become *one* with it, with the Light, with the perfume, with the feelings of oneness, oneness with The Golden Essence, oneness with All There Is, for in this moment of your existence,

YOU ARE GOLDEN,

YOU ARE LIGHT,

YOU ARE LOVE,

YOU ARE ALL THERE IS.

Remember this feeling of floating or flying or being, whatever it is that you have chosen to feel, and *know* that it is always your choice to be wherever it is that you wish to be in The Creation of All There Is.

You may come here to this Field of Golden Essence as often as you like, and remember always that

THE GOLDEN ESSENCE IS YOU.

Remember. Remember. Remember the truth of who you truly *are*. Keep your vision in the forefront of your mind, of yourself as The Golden Essence of All There Is, and know that this is always available to you, and most especially remember that when you are at a level where you can experience The Field of Golden Essence, you **are** in the fifth dimension and beyond.

✖✖✖

And so, we would recommend that you use this simple visualization energy exercise as often as you like, in addition to the meditation we have given you (*The Journey to the Sea of Love and Light*).

The Golden Essence Is YOU

Know that you are deeply loved at all times, by not only us, but by *all* Creation and most especially by The Creator Itself, for you come from The Creator, and to The Creator you will return.

And for this time, the speaking is ended.

We are the Archangels and many, many, many more, and we send you all the Love that we have available, now and always.

CHAPTER SEVENTEEN

A VISIT WITH THE ARCHANGELS

We would like to take you back into *The Field of Golden Essence* that you visited with us yesterday, and we ask you now to return to the breathing pattern of slow and deep.

There is a pathway that leads from the third dimension/fourth dimension forward in front of you. It is filled with LIGHT, and we ask you now to step upon this pathway. You may walk upon it, you may float above it, you may fly, if you like, but set your intention upon the vision of *The Golden Essence* and you will be there. And from this place of *Golden Essence* we will speak with you today.

You may see us in the distance, and we are approaching. As you approach us, we approach you, and as we draw ever closer, you may begin to see many colors flowing forth toward you. We wish to show you our colors today, and appear only as LIGHT and COLOR. We will not appear today in human form as we usually do with humans, for they feel, in general, more comfortable communicating with what they imagine an Angel looks like. We wish to appear to you in our true form: Beings of Light and Color. We each carry all the colors, and we each carry one particular color, and this is the way that those of you upon the Earth think of us, as wearing colors of healing, colors of wisdom, colors of love, colors of protection, the colors that you have learned upon the Earth to associate with these qualities.

There are many colors here today that you will most probably not be able to perceive just yet, but believe us when we say you *will* see them. You will see these most beautiful and unusual colors, which are beyond the so-called physical light spectrum of the Earth in 3D/4D, visible to human eyes, for the colors — many, many, many more colors that are here — cannot be seen by the human eye. They can be seen only by *the inner eye of the heart*, and yes, we say your heart sees; your heart sees as well as thinks, as feels, as knows, for your heart is the center of your being, is it not?

The heart is the Center of All There Is, for Love emanates from the heart and it is the heart of The Creator that sends out LOVE to all Creation. So you may, if you wish, imagine The Creator as an enormous all-encompassing HEART composed of LIGHT and LOVE, and the LOVE, which emanates forth

The Golden Essence Is YOU

from The Creator, is most powerful. It is necessary for The Creator to modulate the energies being sent out: the energies are slowed down gradually so as to protect all of you, and to keep you safe, for if you as a human in human form were to receive a burst of The Original Energy of The Creator, you would disappear instantly in human form, and appear here on this side of the Veil in your Light Form.

We would like to say today that those of you upon the Earth who are able to join us in *The Field of Golden Essence* will all be joining the Earth in the Ascension Process, and so we urge you most gently to disseminate this information we are giving you about the journey to *The Field of Golden Essence.* Tell all you can. Let them hear us speak of it. Lead them in meditation to feel the energies, to smell the perfumes, to know the beauty and the wisdom, which is here in this special place of recognition of The Beauty of The Source, The Creator Light. We wish you to know that those of you, who are able to join us here daily, will advance much more rapidly into and through the Ascension Process.

"*The Field of Golden Essence*" and "*The Journey to the Sea of Love and Light*" are two ways in which to raise your vibratory frequencies more rapidly than usual, for if you are able to see and feel these places — and it becomes easier with practice — you will find it easier to pass through the energies, or to allow the energies which are coming onto the Earth plane to pass through you, with less trauma, with more ease. If, for example, you feel that you in your physical form are becoming tense, perhaps even angry, frustrated, take the time to sit, close your eyes, visualize *The Field of Golden Essence*, breathe in the perfumes, feel the energies, know that you are safe, and always protected. Breathe in the waves of energy, and allow them to just travel through you. You may even pass them down your cords *(The Archangels refer here to "grounding cords"; see Glossary)* into the Earth. You may see yourself as a conduit, receiving, transforming, and passing on the energies of Love which are now coming in greater abundance onto the Earth and through every living being on the Earth, even through the rocks, the waters, the plants, the insects, the animals, the humans, birds, clouds, everything, everything is filling with the Love and the special LIGHT, the very special LIGHT which is coming to you now, coming to the Earth, coming to all of you. Allow it all to flow over you and through you, around and about you, and pass it along to Mother Earth, to Gaia. And in this way, you may remain more calm than you would without a technique to help you.

We ask that you take the time during your day always to visit not only "*The Sea of Love and Light*", but also, at other times, to simply close your eyes and SEE "*The Field of Golden Essence*". Be there. Breathe it in. And breathe out any negative feelings, any negative thoughts, any negativity whatsoever. Breathe in the Light and the Love; breathe out all negativity. You need not do this for a very long period of Earth time, a few minutes is enough, and of course, you may stay there as long as you like, if you have the time and the inclination. We do not limit you in any way. We bring you news, we give you Love, and we are always ready to help and support you in any way.

Remember to ask. Ask always, and you *will* receive whatever it is that is for you, for your highest good as determined by your Higher Self. It would be good for you to communicate with your Higher Self more often. Just check in from time to time. Ask questions if you need to. You will get the answers, most certainly.

We greet you this day with the warmest Love that we can give you upon the Earth, and we gather all around you now, streaming forth our Love into your hearts. See the colors all around, and know that we are here. We are The Beings of Light who speak to you and who love you so very much.

And for today, the speaking is ended.

CHAPTER EIGHTEEN

THE BEING OF LIGHT IN THE HEART;

METHODS OF MANAGING EMOTIONS

We greet you and we say today to begin that you are doing well in representing us as you go about your day upon the Earth. We need to say to those who are hearing these words or reading them on the printed page that this is also a very helpful exercise for them to undertake, and we will now speak directly to you, the listeners, the readers.

Learn to communicate with yourself, with your heart. Imagine that there is a beautiful Being of Light sitting inside your heart. It may take any form that you wish as long as it is a Being of Light and the Purest Love. You may give a name to this Being if you like. We would like for you to communicate daily, if possible, with this Being of Light in your heart. You may ask questions of it, and you will receive answers, depending upon your advancement. It may be possible for you to hear the answers in your heart, in your mind. It may be necessary for you to sit with paper and pencil or pen and write down the questions and allow yourself to write the answers as they come to you.

The more you sit with the Being in your heart, the easier it will become and the more interesting messages you will receive, for this will open the pathway to a dialogue with what is generally called your Higher Self, and once you are connected with your Higher Self, everything becomes easier. You may ask questions, you may have requests, you may treat your Higher Self as that part of you which is in direct communication with God, with The Goddess, with The Creator Source, and so if you feel inclined to chat with The Creator, ask your Higher Self to connect you more firmly with It and with the Higher Realms. Ask your Higher Self for anything that you desire, and if what you desire is in line with your Contract with your Soul, you will receive it.

Learn to communicate with the unseen part of you. Learn to communicate with the Angels. Learn who your Guides are and learn to communicate with them, for it will be necessary that you are able to hear communications from your Higher Self, from your Guides even more clearly than you hear them now. You may call it your intuition, and this is good, but we say to you that your intuition is firmly linked to your Guides, and it is through your intuition that you get information from your Guides. Perhaps it's just a simple nudging to "go this way", or "turn here", or something quite simple, such as "take an umbrella with you" — little things. And eventually the little things give way to larger things until you are in a place where you can receive stronger intuitive nudgings, and even stronger *(intuitive nudgings)*, until you can trust, trust in your Guides, trust in your Higher Self, and most of all, trust in your *self* to make the right decisions for yourself.

As we have said, the Earth is changing, and there are many natural changes happening. They are becoming larger, and we do not wish to alarm you, but we wish you to know what to expect. We ask you most humbly not to imagine something happening to *you*, for, as the Earth draws closer to becoming a fifth-dimensional Being, — and those of you who have chosen to journey along with her, — as this happens, your thoughts will begin to manifest more rapidly, and we urge you to remain calm at all times, secure in the knowledge that you are safe. We urge you to remember to breathe deeply.

If, by chance, you should realize that you are beginning to feel some sort of fears, close your eyes immediately and breathe deeply. Ask for help with your emotions, and it will be given immediately. Know that the deep breathing calms your body, reduces the flow of adrenalin in your bloodstream, and slows your heart down so that it does not beat too rapidly, thereby precipitating more adrenalin being pumped into your bloodstream and more feelings of fear occurring — it is a cycle. The fear prompts the outflowing of the adrenalin from the gland, and the adrenalin coming to the emotional centers and the heart creates more fear.

We are telling you this so that you can become aware that you may stop this cycle at any point by closing your eyes, asking for help, and breathing deeply. We recommend that you practice this at any point in your day when you notice that you may be a bit irritated, as a slight irritation can lead to a greater irritation, and a greater irritation could possibly lead to anger, and anger always contains an element of fear. Then you feel the adrenalin beginning to make you even more angry. It is best, when you notice that small irritation, to close your eyes, and begin to breathe deeply. Withdraw from whatever situation it is that has caused you to feel irritated or frustrated. Know that you have the power over your body, and that you can call upon your cells immediately to slow down. Call upon your adrenal gland itself: "Slow the pumping now — gradually stop the flow of adrenalin outward". Your adrenal glands will hear you, there is no doubt of that, and they will obey you because you are the head of the body corporate, and what you say, goes.

Notice — notice more carefully your feelings. If you wish to keep a log of what is happening with you minute-by-minute, hour-by-hour, you may profit from that, if that is your inclination. Just remember to close your eyes, to stop the external stimuli, give the command to the gland to stop the outflow of the adrenalin, and breathe slowly and deeply until you become calm again.

In this way, you will be able to control your emotions more readily, and when you are sitting there, and you have gained control, you might want to remember the *feelings* from the meditations that you participate in daily. Remember the feelings of peace. Remember the feelings of calm. Remember the feelings of love. And tell yourself, tell all of your cells, tell your adrenal glands

The Golden Essence Is YOU

in particular, "I love you." For when you say these words "I love you", you effect a change in the entire body, a change that is deep in your DNA, a smoothing out of any rough edges and a confidence in each cell of your body that all is well, and that there is no need for alarm. If you take the time to treat the fear impulse in this way, you *will* gradually be able to eliminate it completely, and become more like a Being of Light on this side of the Veil, where fear does not exist.

Fear is a human emotion, and as a human, it is up to you to control it. We can help, if you ask, by sending you more Love from this side of the Veil, and the Love that we send you goes straight to your heart, so center your feelings upon your heart, center your mind upon your heart, center your brain upon your heart, and *know* that at the deepest level, *you are Love*. And so, when you say to yourself, "*I am Love*" or "*I love me*" or "*I love myself*", the love is magnified and the fear vanishes. We ask you to remember this, and to use it as an experiment, if you like. It may seem very simple, but it is deeply effective, and works on all levels of the body, seen and unseen, physical and electrical. You most probably will feel your nerves relaxing, and your muscles relaxing. If you are especially "tuned in", you will feel your brain relaxing, along with all other parts of you.

If you have the need for more love in your life, concentrate your attention upon your heart, and ask to feel the love that resides in there. And when you need more love, come to us and ask, ask us, ask your Guides, ask your Higher Self, ask The Creator Itself: "I need more Love now", and you will feel it flowing into you from all around you. It is as if you are absorbing the Love from every direction.

Breathe in now, and know that we are sending you the greatest Love that we can send from this side of the Veil to you upon the Earth. Breathe it into your heart now. Feel it filling all of your cells, even your hair. Everything is Love, and all of your cells in particular need a daily dose of Love. Every time you breathe, breathe in Love all around you. Every time you eat, see that which you are consuming as pure Love. Every time you drink water and other fluids, see them as pure Love — Love going into Love — Love entering your heart and spreading throughout your entire being. Every thing is Love. And everything that you eat is Love, if you see it as that. It all depends upon your beliefs and your ideas about food, whether or not it is beneficial for you to consume it. You may ask us, your Guides, your Higher Self, The Creator Source of All There Is, to send Love into your food, and it will be so. You must remember to ask for what it is that you desire. If you want the purest water, ask for it. If you want the highest quality food, ask for it. If you want the cleanest air to breathe, ask for it.

Begin to know for yourself that what you express as your desire has an effect upon everything. We call upon you to be more vigilant about yourselves and your bodies. Take good care of them, for they are the gift of The Creator to you so that you may experience all that you are experiencing now in the third and fourth dimensions.

Those of you already experiencing some degree of the fifth dimension will know whereof we speak when we ask you to be very careful with your thoughts. Train yourselves now to monitor your thinking. Make certain that you are able to exert control over your thinking, so that when you *are* in the fifth dimension, you do not create chaos around you, for your thoughts will manifest very quickly, and you may not desire to have some of your thoughts manifest.

So train yourselves to feel and think only Love, to be aware of the goodness in all things. Be aware of the beauty around you, and where there seems not to be beauty, create it with your thoughts, with your hearts. Start practicing now, this creating business. Start practicing now, intending what it is that you wish to see in your world. Begin practicing your creating now, so that when it manifests instantly, you will be pleased and not horrified.

We leave you now and we enfold you in our Light. We wrap our streams of Love around you, and we send you Peace.

And for this time on the Earth, the speaking is ended.

CHAPTER NINETEEN

VISUALIZATION: JOURNEY TO THE WHALES AND THE DOLPHINS

We say to you today that it is always good to remember who you are, and in order for you to refresh your memory, it is good that you participate in either the meditation *"Journey to the Sea of Love"*, or the visualization of *"The Field of Golden Essence"*, or both, if you like, and if that is your desire. These two journeys we have given you will take you deeper and deeper into the Crystalline Structure of your DNA, of your etheric body, of your Light Body, and so are very effective tools for practicing loosening the ties that bind you to the flesh, and eventually allowing you to fly right out of your body and directly into the fifth dimension. Many of you hearing these words and seeing them on the written page will not understand exactly whereof we speak, but we assure you that if you continue also with the meditation, the affirmations, and the visualization of *The Golden Essence*, that you will eventually come to understand what it is that we are telling you. The Earth is changing, and you must change along with her, if you wish to go forward into the fifth dimension and beyond.

We have one other journey that we can offer you, and that is a journey under water to your relatives The Whales and The Dolphins. These are beings of the highest level of vibratory frequency who welcome you always to their realm within the waters of your planet.

✻✻✻

VISUALIZATION: JOURNEY TO THE WHALES AND THE DOLPHINS

If you will, simply close your eyes once more, relax into your chair or whatever it is that you are resting upon, and imagine before you the most beautiful color of deep, deep blue. We ask you to trust us when we say that you are able to enter into this deep blue color in your mind and you will be safe within this deep blue color, for it is there

The Golden Essence Is YOU

in the vibration of BLUE that The Whales meet us.

So come with us now. Know that you are safe. Dispense with the idea of not being able to breathe under water. Just for these next few moments of time on Earth, we journey with you under the water and we keep you safe, because *you can breathe under water* — you have just forgotten your gills. Imagine for a while that you have gills like a fish and that you can take water in and receive oxygen from that water.

Come with us now into the Domain of The Whale, and let us listen to their beautiful songs, their songs of life, their songs of beauty, their songs of Love. You may journey with The Whales wherever it is they wish to take you, and you become aware now of a gigantic Whale next to you who is your guide on this journey. The Whale will lead you, all the while communicating silently to you its story, and you will know what it speaks of, for the message goes straight into your unconscious mind, and as you move through the water gracefully, accompanied by many, many Whales, you will feel a deep sense of wisdom, knowledge, purpose, dignity, and love. The Whales are Love, as you are Love, and as you swim alongside these beautiful creatures, you notice in the distance a lighter color of blue as you swim up closer to the surface of the ocean, and the water is so warm and many different colors of blue, green, blue-green and turquoise. And swimming around you now, joining the Whales, is your family of Dolphins, joyful, happy, playful, enthusiastic, curious, and they too are creatures of Love. They jump and play around you, filling you with their joy, filling you with their happiness, their sense of fun, with their Love, and you understand that everywhere upon your planet there are creatures who are intelligent and who are Love, just as you are intelligent and you are Love. And you realize the responsibility for the well-being of these creatures of the sea lies upon *your* shoulders — that it is up to **you** to protect **them.** It is up to **you** to spread the knowledge of their true essence, which is Love.

The Golden Essence Is YOU

We bring you back now, out of the ocean, and ask you to join us in celebrating the beauty and magnificence of The Whales and the joy and the playfulness of The Dolphins. We ask you to bring all of their qualities back with you as a part of your essence now and know that they are all a part of the same Family of Creation.

❈❈❈

We entrust you with the knowledge that all is well with all of the creatures of Earth, and even though it may feel as if many of them are in danger, in truth they also have their contracts and they are fulfilling them now. We ask you to honor them, love them, and remember always that everything, everything is energy, and when something may *seem* to disappear here upon the Earth, we assure you that it will reappear somewhere else, for energy cannot be destroyed. Energy exists as long as The Creator exists, and that, we can tell you now is *forever.*

The Creator is Eternal. You are Eternal. The animals are Eternal. The Essence of everything is Love, and Love, of course, is Eternal.

We send you our highest vibrations of Love that you can accept at this time. We ask you to open your hearts and allow our Love to flow. Breathe it in and know that WE ARE ALL ONE.

And for this time, the speaking is ended.

NOTES ON THE INFORMATION IN THE FOLLOWING CHAPTER

ABOUT TRIAD PLATFORMS

The Archangels began speaking about Triad Platforms during the time that my husband and I were in the middle of a course that included our mentally making triangles out of specific words, feeling them in our bodies, and using them on a daily basis. This course is called "Mastering Alchemy, Level Two", and is taught by Jim Self. Those of you who may be interested in hearing more about Jim's courses, or perhaps even joining him for his classes, can access this material on his website: www.masteringalchemy.com.

Jim offers free material, as well as information about his courses, on his website. We recommend his work as an adjunct to this book, and, in fact, Jim has a relationship with the Archangels that is very deep; according to Jim, he receives information from them during his nightly forays out-of-body, and he includes the information in his courses.

CHAPTER TWENTY

NOW TIME;
TRIAD PLATFORMS;
CORD-CUTTING

We welcome you today, and we would like to say to begin that the time that you take to listen to us exists fully and completely in NOW TIME, and we wish to remind you that after we finish speaking today, it would be good for you to practice remaining in NOW TIME, since, as you know, the past is the past, and the future is the "now" which is coming to you, but which you create with every breath and every thought and every emotion you experience in this moment now of NOW TIME.

It is important for you that you remain as much in NOW TIME as you are capable of, so that you can be an example for others of the way in which the most effective life on this planet at this time can be lived, and that is completely in the NOW, creating as you go along, not thinking of the next minute or the next hour or the next day, but remaining completely *present* and *open* and *excited* and *creative*, and these platforms that Jim (Jim Self) is giving you of the words are very important for maintaining the "time" of the NOW. Choose the words that you wish to use every day, and we say to you also that it is not imperative to choose simply three words for one day, but you may choose three words for every minute, if you like, changing them as you go along, feeling the words, feeling the vibrations of the words is most important, and if you wish, you may make a meditation around the words.

Take five minutes, for example, and feel the combinations of words. *Feel* them and *know* them in the NOW. For example, if you would now take the time to feel, for example, HAPPY. And feel that feeling fully and completely, without imagining anything that makes you happy, or anything that might make you happy in the future, or anything that has made you happy in the past. Just *feel* the vibrations of HAPPY now — HAPPY, HAPPY, HAPPIER. *Feel* the HAPPY until you know there is a smile upon your face, and that you *feel* the excitement of the word HAPPY, for there is a deep excitement bound to the vibrational process of hearing the sounds of HAPPY in your language.

It can also affect you in the same way in another language, even though the word may be different. For example, the French

The Golden Essence Is YOU

"JOYEUX". "JOYEUX" feels the same to a French-speaking person as "HAPPY" does to you. It may not feel the same to *you*, it may feel close to what you feel when you feel happy, but we tell you that in every language, the word that means "HAPPY" to you also creates a similar vibration for all of the people speaking the other languages on your planet.

We say also today that a good combination for you to make with HAPPY is CAPABLE. CAPABLE. Feel the feelings surrounding the word CAPABLE. CAPABLE and HAPPY go very well together. And CAPABLE and HAPPY may need a word which is a bit stabilizing, and in that case, we might suggest that you choose a word which has a more masculine vibration, such as CONFIDENT — CONFIDENT — a very angular word, a very stabilizing word, very masculine in its feelings of creating a solid platform for CAPABLE and HAPPY. CAPABLE, HAPPY, CONFIDENT!

Feel the feelings of the word CONFIDENT, the *knowing* that is inherent in those syllables, CON – FI – DENT, CONFIDENT. The word CONFIDENT is softened somewhat by pairing it with HAPPY — HAPPY and CONFIDENT — quite beautiful vibrations, and CONFIDENT and CAPABLE are a combination which is unbeatable.

So you see, the exercise which you have learned of pairing these Triads of Words can be very beneficial for you, and certainly when you journey to the fifth dimension and beyond, the vibrational rates of those words will carry you higher and give you a greater ability to create what it is that you wish to create, and to maintain your thought processes in an organized way so that you are not totally confused and creating many, many things at once, with your thoughts jumping about.

> *(The following information was given as a personal message to the Co-author and her husband, but this paragraph is very important for all of you, and it is therefore included.)*
>
> "Learning to create various Triad Platforms for you to rely upon in the fifth dimension and beyond is quite beneficial, and we would recommend that when you are practicing, you try out many combinations, different, unusual combinations of words using the words that you have in your list *(reference to Jim Self's Level Two course)* and also coming up with your own combinations of words which may *not* be on your list, but which may be also *very* beneficial for you personally. We do not recommend that you jump ahead of what you are learning with Jim, but you could try out a few other words not on the list, just to see what happens to your feelings in NOW TIME."

We say to those of you who are not familiar with the Triad Platforms, that we do not wish to take away from the teachings that we have given to Jim, but we recommend that you contact him directly in order to decide for yourselves whether or not you wish to become a master of alchemy also.

We would like to say now that any path you choose which creates harmonious vibrations for you and helps you to speed up the rate of your vibrations, of your vibrational frequencies, any path is good that leads you towards the Higher Realms of Light and of Love.

The more you can bring your own emotional development into alignment with that of the Ascended Masters, the Council of Light, The All There Is, the Angelic Realm, — everything you can do to make yourselves in physical form, or to create yourselves anew in physical form, in this direction is good. If you hear of something new, and you'd like to try it, by all means, try it. However, if you find, that after trying it, you feel exactly the same as you did *before* you tried it, or in some cases, not as good as you felt before you tried it, we would recommend that you would examine this very carefully, and make your own decision about whether or not this new "toy" is appropriate for you. We cannot tell you what to do and what not to do; we can recommend only that if you have doubts about anything, *ask your Higher Self,* for your Higher Self is that interface between you, the human, and everything else on the other side of the Veil, where we are, for example, where the Ascended Masters are, where the Council of Light is, where every Being is who is not in human, physical form at this time in the NOW upon the Earth is.

We recommend to you that you use some form of meditation daily, be it five minutes or twenty-five minutes, it matters not. If you can achieve a deep, deep, deep level of slow brain wave that allows you to interface with us, with others on this side of the Veil, with anyone here whom you would like to contact, if you can do that in five minutes, brilliant. If it takes you twenty-five minutes, also brilliant. We do not praise those of you more who are able to do it quickly, and we do not praise those of you more who are not so quick. Everyone is on his or her, or we might say, in terms of *here*, <u>its</u> own pathway, and whatever you choose for yourself, in any of your existences, anywhere, any time, is your own personal matter.

We do not interfere, the Ascended Masters do not interfere, the Council of Light does not interfere — no one interferes with your choices — no one. And we remind you once more: should you ever need help, you need only ask for it, for whatever you ask will be granted, if it is within your Life Plan and your Contract with your Soul. And even then, contracts can be changed.

This is a more complex process that we will not go into now, but we say to you: if there is some part of your Contract, and you know your Contract, and are able to access all of the details through your Higher Self, through your Guides, through us, through a reader of the Akasha — if you find something in your Contract that is not what you wish now in NOW TIME, you may request a change, and if it is appropriate, it will be changed. This is something that must be discussed with your Higher Self, with your Guides, with your Soul, and you can ask anyone to help you. If you are absolutely certain that a part of your Contract is holding you back in any way, you may ask to change it. Believe us when we say this.

We say to you now that it is still extremely important to cut the cords of attachment, which you have placed into other beings on the Earth, or elsewhere, or that other beings elsewhere or on the Earth have placed into you. And, as we have said before, if they are not meant to be cut, they will re-attach.

The Golden Essence Is YOU

There are occasions when, if you are not *very* clear with the person with whom you are attached that you are cutting the cords *permanently*, they may attempt to re-attach to you, and if you are open and have neglected to say, "No more attachments with this person", they may be able to re-attach, in which case, you need to go again, consult with your Higher Self, have your Higher Self consult with *their* Higher Self, and make certain that it is not necessary for you to be attached before you cut the cords. If it is absolutely certain that you need to cut, then cut again.

If there is some reason — and we will not go into detail now what those reasons might be — if there is some reason why a cord or cords must be between you and another being, and you have spoken with your Higher Self about this, and received the recommendation that you remain attached, and you may receive an "Attachment Notice" for a certain period of Earth time, in which case at the end of the "Attachment Notice" period of time, you go back, consult the Higher Selves, and cut the cords again, if that is what is needed.

One exception we will make now, and that is to say that if there is a certain Master Teacher you are working with, those cords may remain attached, for a Master Teacher, or a Master, has an extremely high vibratory level, and it is beneficial for you to receive the vibrations from this teacher until that time at which you will have reached the higher level of vibratory frequencies, and your vibrations match those of the teacher. In that case, the cords may be cut, but up until that point, it is beneficial for you to remain attached. You may check with your Higher Self to see if there are cords of attachment between you and the Master Teacher that are not necessary, in which case, you may cut those, but the major cords of the very high vibrational frequency should remain in place, as we have said.

And so we urge you now to consider everything that we have said today: Work with the platforms of the words, work with remaining in NOW TIME for this complete day, if it is possible, and gently pull yourself back from the future, if that is the most pulling that you receive.

Also, if you are cutting cords today, make certain that you can bring the person you are consulting with about cutting cords into *your* NOW TIME. Do not go back to the *past* where you connected the cords; bring that person's image before you in the *now*. See them in the *now*. If you cannot see them in the *now*, leave it for today, and go to someone else. Remember to remain in the NOW at all times — it is very important.

And for now, the speaking is ended.

CHAPTER TWENTY-ONE

TRIAD PLATFORMS

We greet you this day, and we ask you now to take a few moments to prepare a platform for yourselves, which will allow you to accept the energies flowing onto the Earth now more powerfully. These energies need to be brought in and stabilized. We would suggest that you might consider using the word PEACEFUL, the word ACCEPTING, and the word LOVE, for these three words in combination — PEACEFUL, ACCEPTING, LOVE — will help you in the assimilation of the energies flowing inward into both of you and into everyone on the Earth plane today. So if you would take a moment and visualize a triangular platform below your feet through which the energy from Mother Earth flows upward into your Column of Light *(the center core of your body),* and on corners of this platform are the words written in *gold*: PEACEFUL, ACCEPTING, LOVE. And in this way, you will more easily be able to allow the energies coming through and onto the Earth to flow through you.

We ask you to breathe into your hearts and receive the energies that we are sending to you, the energies of Peace, the energies of Love, the energies of The All There Is. These energies are flowing quite strongly today, especially today, and we wish for you to be able to interact with one another, remembering always the words, the vibrations of the words, and if you have already chosen three words for yourself for this day, that is good. You may combine them with the three which we have suggested.

There is no limit to the number of words you may wish to have on your platforms. There is no limit to the number of platforms that you may have. Think of the Grid around the Earth, and imagine your Triad Platforms surrounding yourself and protecting you in a way, both from outside influences and from anything within yourself, which might be discordant, or limiting, or negative.

We ask you to remember always the Light. Keep the Light within, see the Light within your hearts, and spread it out throughout your bodies and outward beyond your bodies into your etheric bodies, into your entire energy field. Become a Being of Light upon the Earth, and know that everything you do, everything you say, everything you feel, everything you sense, everything you think, affects everything else, and yourself.

Know that it is important to maintain your own integrity and to clear out all limiting beliefs as soon as possible, all memories that may be limiting, and all feelings that may still be painful. We urge you to use whatever means at your disposal to bring your bodies, your senses, your feelings, your thinking into balance, into alignment, so that your activities may be joyful for you and your interactions with others loving and kind.

We see that you are challenged by the energies flowing onto the Earth, and we wish for you to be aware that everything is as it is supposed to be and that you are perfect. We give you information about the assimilation of the energies so that you may help others who are having much more difficulty than you are with understanding what is happening to them and around them.

We ask you to remember always your origins as Sparks of The Creator Itself, sent forward and outward into the Universe to experience all that you can experience and to learn from the experiences what it is that you wish to learn. Know that you are the captains of your own ships and you can choose to sail comfortably or you can choose other alternatives. We know that you are searching and growing, and that growing sometimes is uncomfortable, and we say to you, "Keep breathing" when you feel uncomfortable. Breathe deeply, and allow your body processes to slow down, just enough so that the uncomfortable feeling is stretched out a bit, and when *discomfort* is stretched out, further and further and further, you begin to lose the "*dis*" part and you begin to experience more of the "*comfort*" part.

Know that you can always turn one sensation or situation into another; it is always a matter of choosing which direction you wish to go, which direction you wish to sail on your ship. You can sail toward the sunrise or you can sail toward the sunset. You can sail away from the stormy seas, and you can sail into the storm. You can choose sunlight, and you can choose shadow. You can choose happy as well as unhappy. Remember that your life is a wonderful opportunity to discover how *choosing* a course of action helps you to create your life. Choosing to go forward or choosing to stand still. Choosing to be calm or choosing to be agitated. There are so many possibilities, and we understand when you feel it is necessary to choose something other than PEACE, something other than LOVE, something other than UNDERSTANDING.

We understand very well the difficulties of experiencing life in human form upon your planet of free choice, and many of you find it extremely difficult to make the choices that you want to feel are "right", but we say to you that nothing is "right" or "wrong", that everything is your experience as you choose to create it in a certain moment of time, NOW TIME. When you create in NOW TIME, you see the results in NOW TIME, for as you know, and we have said, there is no past, there is no future, there is *only* NOW. It would be good to remember that you live fully *only* in the NOW, and the other living that you do, thinking about the past, projecting about the future — that is not living. That is something that you choose to do in order to "tread water", to waste time, to avoid being present, to avoid being in the NOW, to avoid *living*. There are often fears behind this behavior, and we suggest that, if you can dig a little deeper and find out what the fears are, then you may begin to eliminate them, one by one.

Bringing *fear* into the *Light* is a great step forward on the path to Ascension. You would not wish to arrive in the fifth

The Golden Essence Is YOU

dimension filled with fear, would you? It is most beneficial for all of you to dig deeply, find your fears, confront them, find the "Creation Factor" behind them, and work with your Higher Self to change the fears into something positive. Or you can completely eliminate the fear, which does not serve you, and during this entire process, it is good to remember that you are safe, that we are here also, to help you, if you *ask*, and that The Creator, of course, is constantly streaming forth Its energies of Love and Light in all directions and most especially to those of you who ask for help.

We say to you now that the sun is always shining somewhere, why not inside of *you*? Acknowledge that you are a Being of Light and of Love and that your creations will from now forward be filled with that essence of you, with Light and with Love.

We enfold you now in our streams of wing-like Light. We stream forth to you our Love into your hearts. Open your hearts just a bit wider to receive the Love that we have for you, that we feel so deeply for you, and that will always, always be available to you. Be well this day. Journey forward on your platform of LOVE, PEACE, and ACCEPTING, ALLOWING, HONORING — any words, really and truly, that you feel that you wish to stand upon today and in any time of discomfort or pain, allowing everything to flow into you, through you, back to The Creator, and down to Mother Earth.

And for this time, the speaking is ended.

CHAPTER TWENTY-TWO

MEETING YOUR HIGHER SELF

Those of you who come to this information: We ask you to spend a little extra time with the material we are presenting and also away from the material we are presenting, in reflection, examination of your innermost self, most particularly your belief systems, and work to change any of this that you deem to be of a negative nature. Releasing negativity is extremely important at this period of time.

Releasing the ties that bind you to others is most important at this time, and we urge you to begin immediately with the cutting of the cords, for it does take some of your NOW TIME to accomplish this, following the directives that we have given.

Also, we wish you to forge a tighter connection, a better connection, a more sturdy connection with your Higher Self, so that you may communicate quickly with your Higher Self in a flowing manner so that the information or questions that you might have reaches your Higher Self quickly and the answers come back to you immediately, of course, for your Higher Selves know no time. They exist in the NOW, the ETERNAL NOW, which is why we have urged you to become aware of NOW, for you must contact your Higher Self in the NOW TIME.

It might perhaps be good for us to lead you into a direct communication with your Higher Self at this time.

✿✿✿

VISUALIZATION: MEETING YOUR HIGHER SELF

And so we ask you now to take a deep, slow breath. Center your mind within your heart, and imagine yourself sitting in a beautiful, golden chamber, a room within your heart. You are sitting in the special room where you may meet with your Higher Self, and we say to you now, "Call upon your Higher Self to come into the room with you". And your Higher Self will come.

The Golden Essence Is YOU

You may imagine your Higher Self in any form that you desire, for your Higher Self is capable of changing form at any time. You may recognize your Higher Self by the golden color that it will exhibit, so as soon as you see within your mind's eye, or sense, or feel, within your heart a Being with the vibrational frequency of *gold*, you may then ask that being, "Who are you?" And that being must answer truthfully, who or what it is, and if you are truly tuned in and sensing and feeling and seeing on the appropriate level of your brain waves centered in your heart, that Being will answer back to you that it is the Eternal part of you which is in communication with The Source of All There Is, or something similar. It may call itself "I am your Higher Self"; it may say "I am that Spiritual Being with whom you may communicate all questions and answers", but know that if any other being appears to you who does *not* say that it is of a spiritual dimension or of the capacity to answer questions, then communicate with The Source. You may not yet have reached the proper level of mind, the proper brain wave frequency, to achieve communication.

In this case, we recommend that you breathe more deeply and slowly and that you call on us to help you to communicate with your Higher Self, and once you have reached the proper brain wave frequency level, we will make you acquainted — or perhaps better said — help you to acknowledge your Higher Self within your heart.

So, continue the deep, slow breathing until you have reached the frequency that is necessary to sense, feel, see, or know that your Higher Self is present, and it is in this relaxed, deeply relaxed, state of being that you may communicate with your Higher Self, for the Higher Self is of a much higher vibration than you personally, as a human, can ever reach in human form, and you must create the proper atmosphere within the portion of your being that is already of a higher vibrational level, and that is your Heart Center. From this level you may communicate with your Higher Self, and we say to you that the more rapidly you create a higher vibrational body for yourself, the easier it will be for you to

The Golden Essence Is YOU

communicate with your Higher Self, and for your Higher Self to communicate with you.

✖✖✖

There are some of you who recommend the use of a pendulum for contacting the Higher Self, and for some of you this is good, but we say that for the majority of humans on this Earth there are various parts of your personality beings which can manipulate a pendulum to the personally desired answer and the personally desired effect and not necessarily the truth of the Higher Self. We caution you to be most careful in this area.

It is preferable that you establish a connection within your mind, within your heart, so that you can be absolutely certain that the Being you contact is neither your subconscious mind, nor your unconscious mind, nor your ego self, but that true spiritual Being which is a part of *you* existing on this side of the Veil, and who is allowed to communicate with you at all times.

So anything and everything that you can do to raise your vibrational level and help yourself to become able to reach a deeper and deeper level of brain wave frequency is good. You need to slow your brain waves down to at least the theta, lower theta level, in order to speak with a being of a high frequency, such as that of a Higher Self. You need to be in a deep, trance-like state.

So we ask you to take the time to sit quietly with yourself — five minutes to begin — to clear your mind, breathe deeply, and imagine yourself traveling inward into your heart, and within your heart is that part of you which is your connection to The Source. The Source lives within your heart, and your Higher Self is, of course, a part of The Source, as are we, as are you.

And so we say that whenever you wish to accomplish something of a very spiritual nature, and you have questions, we refer you to your Higher Self, for your Higher Self is that part of you which is eternal, and which is always in communication with The Source of All There Is, with your history, with everything that there is to know about you. Your Higher Self knows everything. You may ask any questions that you like, and you will receive answers. Be not concerned if you do not *hear* answers; you may simply have a *feeling* of what is right for you, of what is the answer to your question.

You may sense it; you may perhaps like to put pen to paper and do what is often called "automatic writing". We caution you here also that there is a possibility, similar to that with the pendulum, that you may be receiving answers from a different source than the one you asked. So be very careful with automatic writing and with the pendulum, for you personally may be answering your own question, and you may not yet, at that point, have achieved true communion with your Higher Self. If you work diligently every day, it will quickly become easier.

We say to you that your Higher Self waits for your questions and is ready to serve at all times. Your Higher Self is also the communication agent, if you will, communication factor, the communication officer between yourself and others on this side of the Veil, including The Source of All There Is. It is not given to all of you to be able to communicate with your senses, with your hearing, with your feelings, with your knowing, with The All There Is, but The All There Is communicates with your Higher Self, and so it is for this reason that we ask you to establish the connection well, for you will be directly accessing The Source through your Higher Self. All of the knowledge, all of the feelings, all of the senses, all of the knowing of The Source is available to you through your Higher Self.

And so it is that we leave you now, temporarily, and we send you our love always, and our wishes for a most beautiful day upon the Earth.

And for this day the speaking is ended.

CHAPTER TWENTY-THREE

ADDITIONAL INFORMATION ABOUT CORD-CUTTING

We greet you this day, and we would say to begin that maintaining a Triad Platform is very beneficial for establishing the parameters of what it is that you need to have before going into the fifth dimension.

We suggest that if you choose words, which together form any sort of a combination that is troublesome or difficult for you during the day, that you simply choose three *different* words, and work with feeling the vibrations of those three words. Everything that you do to advance yourselves to the fifth dimension should flow easily, and if it does not, seek another way to find an exercise or a method (or the words), which does flow easily for you. There may be a reason why you might have some challenges with using certain combinations of words, which will vanish over a period of two to three weeks, and you can go back to the words you have chosen that were a bit difficult and use them again to measure how you have progressed, for they most certainly should feel easier after you have done other work.

It is necessary now for us to remind you yet again that one of the most important exercises you can do is to begin cutting cords of the ties that bind, if you have not already started, and if you have started and stopped for some reason, to take it up again and continue until you have finished. Many of you have met many people in your lives who may have set cords into you without your knowledge, and you may have done so to others without your knowledge, conscious knowledge, and it is for this reason that it is important to begin cutting and continue until you can think of no one else that you may have met who might have had reason to desire to keep a closer connection with you, or with whom you might desire to have a closer connection.

And we tell you also that you may have cords of connection with people you have *never* met, but whom you have admired, such as, for example, The President of the United States or of any other country, a philanthropist, a well-known investor — anyone whom you admire deeply. It would be good to examine, to see them standing before you, and examine to see if there is a connection on any of the chakra levels, and to cut them now. There may be any number of well-known or even famous personalities — actors, singers, performers of any kind, artists in all fields of endeavor — there are beings who stand out above the rest and who are admired by many. If you feel particularly drawn closer to a personage of fame or of achievement, it would be good to examine to see if there is a closer connection than you actually thought. These are areas that we bring out simply because it might not occur to some of you that there are possible connections and ties between you and people you have not met, but of whom you know and have read about in your public media or have seen performing in some way, so it is good to add these personages to your list of possible connections and to cut the cords with them as well, if you find connections.

When you have reached the end of your list and you are certain that you have cut all the cords of beings with whom you have found that you had connections, you may, with the help of your Higher Self, issue a "blanket statement" of some sort, asking that all other connections between you and persons living or dead, (so-called "dead", i.e., not on the Earth plane any longer), that these cords all be cut, ones that you do not know of but which exist. In this way, we can be certain that you will be completely free to advance to the fifth dimension and beyond, without feeling tied to someone or something on the Earth plane or on this side of the Veil.

We will keep this message for today short, as we see that our messenger wishes it to be, and so we greet you this day and we fold you in our Love and healing energies. We are the Archangels, and these are our truths for this day upon the Earth.

CHAPTER TWENTY-FOUR

NOW TIME;
TRIAD PLATFORMS;
MIRACLES

SUNDAY, VALENTINE'S DAY

We greet you this day, and say to begin that we wish for both of you a beautiful day upon the Earth in NOW TIME, and we will continue on now with the information that we were giving the last Earth period that we spoke *(previous message, Chapter Twenty-Three)*.

We would like for you to remember that the idea of "time" is, or can be, extremely confusing for some, in that the concept of NOW TIME has not been taught in your Earth schools, and those of you who have advanced in your metaphysical or spiritual training, so to speak, of course, have gained some insights into "time" and the way in which it functions, most importantly, that it was created by all of you by consensus upon the Earth that there would be something called "time", which would allow you to have a sense of events happening and then passing into what you call "the past" — very appropriate name — and the anticipation of events in the time to come, which you have called in your English language "the future", and so you understand that there is, in the third dimension, the concept of "past", "present" — what we call "NOW TIME" — and "future".

What we have been attempting to convey to you is the concept that there is actually *no* "time" away from the Earth, and that "time" is that which you call the "fourth dimension", and the fourth dimension is something we can elaborate upon later. But going back to the concept of "time", and NOW TIME in particular, we would like to say that it is most important for you to understand that it is most beneficial for you to remain in the *now*, in the time that is happening *right now*, not to project yourselves into what you call "the future", for then you are not existing in NOW TIME, but in some nebulous area of the fourth dimension which contains pictures of what *may* be coming to you. It's not always accurate when you see these pictures, but your planning area is in the fourth dimension in the "Time Area", and when you close your eyes and travel there, or you go there in your thoughts to plan some — what you call "future event", it takes you away from the present time, and you are not totally within your bodies, and the only way to remain completely grounded and within your body is to access NOW TIME.

The Golden Essence Is YOU

So in the case of desiring to ascend to the fifth dimension, you must realize that it is very important that you understand the concept of "time" or lack of time, "no time" or NOW TIME, NOW TIME being that which you are experiencing *right now* at this very second, from second-to-second, mini-second-to-mini-second, from nano-second-to-nano-second as you are listening, and not allowing your mind to wander, or reading and not allowing your mind to wander, or listening to what we have to say about "time".

We want to impress upon you the importance of remaining totally present in your body, experiencing NOW TIME, creating your platforms of the important words and feeling them in NOW TIME, not *pretending* to feel them in the future, at some point in the future, but to actually spend NOW TIME examining the words that we have talked with you about and which were introduced by Jim Self to you *(the Co-Author and her husband)*, and there is information at the end of the book about how to contact Jim and receive more information about the words. In any case, we digress.

We go back now to NOW TIME, and by going back, we do not imply in any way that we are going into "the past". We are returning to NOW TIME from a digression, with some information for you. And so we say: Allow the past to be the past, and spend *no time* there if you can possibly arrange it. We know that some memories are very beautiful and it is very pleasant to dream about re-experiencing certain beautiful events that have occurred in your life, or in your lifetimes, for if you search with a facilitator, or on your own, for past lifetimes, as you call them on Earth, you may find some parts of that time, but it takes a great deal of finesse, knowledge, and capability to access a lifetime which you may be living simultaneously in the NOW.

So we say to you that there are holograms of an entire lifetime, which you are living in another dimension, NOW, and we will not go into that, but we can say that you may access the holograms and see the entire lifetime from beginning to end. We realize that this is extremely confusing, for you have created "time", with past, present, and future, and so you imagine that the past, so-called, lifetimes are existing in "the past" because you know that there was a birth into some form of life in the third dimension, or possibly elsewhere, if you are able to access any of those memories, on other planetary systems, in other star systems, and we will not talk about that either now, but go back to the concept of the "past lives".

The holograms are there for all of you to experience: past, present, future, in Earth terms. But in truth, you are experiencing these what we will call "other lifetimes" in the NOW, and we urge you not to spend a great deal of time confusing yourselves, or becoming confused because of the difficulty of imagining how this actually functions.

This is not a function of third-dimensional existence, and so it is rather difficult for you to comprehend this at this time, but we assure you that once you have ascended, and you are able to reach the fifth dimension and beyond, this will all become extremely clear to you. And so, we mention it now so that you will be prepared, and you will know that other lifetimes are events that are visible to you here, if you are able to access them, and *seem* to have occurred in your past.

The Golden Essence Is YOU

There are, however, others of you who have already experienced a *"future"* lifetime, as you call it, which is simply another hologram of something that is not accessible to you in any other concept except as being of the "future", and not of the "past", and we know, and we apologize if this is extremely confusing to you, but we feel that it is necessary for you to understand or to at least *hear* the information, even if you do not yet understand it, and we urge you also to remain PRESENT, CAPABLE, and CALM when contemplating these ideas. So experience the Triad Platform of PRESENT, CAPABLE, and CALM when you are confronted or presented with new concepts and ideas that are possibly difficult for you to understand. That is all, and we wish for you to know this information.

We will say now that the time is coming even more rapidly upon the Earth in NOW TIME, when events are advancing much more rapidly than those of you who understand what is transpiring have expected, and to those of you who are encountering these concepts for the first time, by reading or listening to this information, this is possibly a confusing area for you and we ask you to just simply *feel* the words, *feel* the vibrations of the words — CALM — remain CALM when confronted with new information. You might also choose to put in there the vibrational frequencies of UNDERSTANDING. CALM and UNDERSTANDING allow you to access new information without fear, so if you are UNDERSTANDING and CALM and OPEN, open to new information, but OPEN is simply the word that you would feel. You feel CALM, you feel OPEN to new information, for example, and UNDERSTANDING. So

CALM, OPEN, and UNDERSTANDING are very important vibrational frequencies for you to feel when you are presented with new information.

We give you some of these concepts of the three words joined together which we have termed "Triad Platforms" — you may call it "Triad Utility" if you like, if "Platform" seems a bit odd, but "Triads", in any case, of words that contain very different vibrational frequencies. If you sit now, for example, as you are sitting, or standing — whichever it is that you have chosen — and feel the vibrations of this word: VINDICATION. VINDICATION. VINDICATION carries with it a vibrational frequency, which is a powerful frequency of KNOWING. KNOWING that something that you have accomplished *is* and *was*, if you want to use your past term, but *"is"* is our preferred word. VINDICATION is a word which contains the frequency of accomplishing something that may have been — "attacked" is not the correct word here — but implies that another person has doubted something that you have attempted to accomplish.

In any case, VINDICATION carries with it the frequency of ACCOMPLISHMENT, and so VINDICATION is a very powerful word, as we have said, and the feeling of ACCOMPLISHMENT goes along with that, and so, if you wish to combine VINDICATION with ACCOMPLISHMENT and HAPPY, then of course, you have two feelings that are similar but not the same, joined with a very light-hearted, wonderful feeling vibration of joyousness, of happiness, of HAPPY. Be HAPPY. So along with VINDICATION and HAPPY, you feel the feelings of ACCOMPLISHMENT. These three words may be very helpful to you in some situations that you might encounter. And so on it goes with the three words.

We are emphasizing the three words in more than one section of the book because the words are very important for you when you arrive in the fifth dimension, and if anything is confusing to you at any time, even *now* or in the fifth dimension, or on the way *to* the fifth dimension, you can immediately call upon some of your stabilizing words and feel the vibrations of, for example, STABILITY — STABILITY — very firm, wonderful feeling of grounded, groundedness, firmness, being on the Earth, being *of* the Earth. STABILITY. CAPABLE and STABILITY go very well together. You are CAPABLE, you have STABILITY, and VISION. You have VISION. Or you are VISIONARY, SEEING. So these three words are very interesting combinations.

We urge you to look for your own combinations of words that will help you to accomplish more in your life, even now as you are working towards the fifth dimension. Do not look at it as something in the future, for it is already in your "now". It is just not yet visible to you. The aspects of it can be accessed through a journey with your eyes closed, and we recommend that you perhaps check in with Jim Self, or contact Jim Self for more information about visiting the fifth dimension.

We speak now of how you might wish to live your life in the *now* upon planet Earth, where you are *now*, and are experiencing great upheavals in all aspects of third-dimensional life, are you not? There is the financial instability of the world markets, there are the Earth changes, which are not huge at this point, but some of them are very big — the earthquakes, the snowstorms, the rainstorms, the mud — many things that are making life rather extremely difficult for some of you upon the Earth.

And this brings to mind one other aspect of the three-word combinations, or The Triad Platforms. If you have some apprehensions or fears about Earth changes occurring near you, choose WELL-BEING — WELL-BEING, and SAFETY, or SAFE, as in "I am SAFE", "I have a sense of WELL-BEING", — and deep breathing. Both of these words will tend to begin a process within your body of calming you down in the case of fears, which might be brought up at the idea of a disaster of a large earthquake, for example, or a tsunami with the oceans, if you live near the ocean, tornadoes, windstorms, mudslides, large amounts of snow, large amounts of rain — all of these types of activities that Mother Earth is experiencing now in greater frequency and in larger dimensional aspect.

If you begin to have feelings of fear, as we have said, sit down somewhere, close your eyes, begin the slow, deep breathing, know that you are SAFE, know that WELL-BEING is a part of your platform. SAFETY, WELL-BEING and CALM are three excellent words, and we say that you always have the choice to choose the three words which best suit *you* in their vibrational frequencies, for your vibrational frequency must match with the frequencies of the three words in order for them to be effective for you.

For example, if you are already in overwhelming fear, perhaps CALM is not the correct word for you. WELL-BEING and SAFETY combined with GOD'S LOVE may be the most appropriate combination, for if you are already extremely fearful, the adrenalin is flowing within your bloodstream, as we have said. You need to CALM this area, and remembering that The Creator, The Source of All There Is, loves you beyond measure and wishes for you that which you wish for yourself, which may be SAFETY, which may be PROTECTION, which may be any of the positive words which can help slow your heartbeat, for if you are in a panic situation, your heart is beating quite rapidly, you will be, possibly you *are*, let us remain in NOW TIME — you are hyperventilating and you are extremely fearful. Breathing slowly is the best for this type of situation. Reminding yourself that you are *LOVE,* that you are *LOVED,* that you *ARE* love and that you *ARE* loved and that you may at any time call upon your Higher Self to help you in any sort of situation. Remember these things. Place them at the front of your mind. *Know* that you are SAFE, *know* that you are PROTECTED, *know* that you are choosing to be in the right place at the right time, which is *now* during any sort of natural calamity, natural occurrence, natural catastrophe, even.

There are many stories on your planet of, for example, being on an airplane that crashes. We do not wish to bring up fear in any of you, but there have been stories of all beings on an aircraft *except one* leaving the Earth together, and the *one* survives, because the *one* who survives has a contract to remain upon the Earth, and nothing can cause it to leave and come back to this side of the Veil until it has reached its goals and has accomplished everything that it wishes to accomplish upon the Earth in that particular body, at which time it may choose to come Home of its own free will. Some occurrence may happen that will cause it to understand it is time to leave, and something will come up that will help it along. There are many stories in the history of Earth of beings who have survived, and you call them "Miracles".

There have recently been, in your Earth history in the first two months of the year 2010, in the country called Haiti, there have been "miracles" of beings, human beings, found under the rubble even one month after the earthquake. One month! This is almost unbelievable for many of you, for this current knowledge, the current information about how long a human may live without water, without food, is not a very long time, but you have seen the miraculous rescues of people after two weeks, after three weeks, and even recently, after *one month*. You see, there are Contracts with your Souls that will and must be fulfilled, and if you have not planned to leave the Earth, you will not leave. You will be found. And we hesitate to use the words "will be", but that is for those of you in the third dimension who understand this language best, and it implies a future event from the time of the beginning of the disaster, for example.

We urge you whenever possible, to consider yourselves in NOW TIME, and spend all of your time that you can in NOW TIME. You may have to speak with another person about an appointment in the so-called "future", and that is all well and good. We understand that there are appointments which must be made for certain things, but do not dwell upon them. Make the appointment. Write it down. Know that it will happen in NOW TIME when that date arrives, and that is quite simple. We do not need to go on about that.

The Golden Essence Is YOU

But we do say to you that the Three-Word Platforms, the Triad Platforms, and the NOW TIME go together. It is impossible for you to *feel* The Triads in the "past". It is impossible for you to *feel* The Triads in the "future", for the "future" is a timeline of events that have not yet happened in the *now*. The only place that you can *feel* the vibrational frequencies of The Triad Platforms is in the *now*. And so, in order for you to practice these very important vibrational frequency words, you must be *in*, and experiencing, NOW TIME.

We would like to say also that continuing to cut the cords is very important, but we have already expounded upon this, and we will not dwell on it at this time. Remember to search out, and in this case, you *may* have to go into the "past" to remember people with whom you have become acquainted and with whom you might possibly have cord connections. We understand that this part of cord-cutting, which happens in the *now*, essentially comes from the "past", from your memories. And so, it is good to delve into your memory banks in order to find the names, but understand that the entire process of cutting the cords, of course, happens in NOW TIME.

And so we say to you: Be not concerned about future events upon the Earth. Everything happens because of the Contracts with the Souls of the beings upon the Earth who are impacted by them. Everything happens because of the Contracts with the Souls. We wish you to understand this concept, as we know many of you ask, "Why? Why does this happen? Why does this happen to that person? Why does this happen to that baby? Why does this happen to these soldiers?" And we say to you it is all within *their* Life Plans.

Their Contracts with their Souls are composed in order for them to gain certain experiences.

If we can help you to understand one thing it is this: There are no tragedies. There are no disasters. There are no horrific events, even though they may seem so to you. We assure you that everything is within the Soul's Plan, even bodily suffering, even bodily suffering. For we know that many of you will have known, or do know, human beings who have suffered with diseases of a long and painful nature. And this sometimes seems incomprehensible that what you call "God" would allow such a thing, and we say to you that God, Goddess, The Creator Source of All There Is understands and feels all of the pain; all of the pain which is experienced by all of you is felt even more deeply by your God, your Goddess, your Source, your Creator, and The Source does not interfere where there is a Contract to experience the pain for the growth of the soul. We know this is difficult for you, for pain is an unwelcome part of human existence and the result of your highly developed nervous systems.

We say to you now that we love you beyond belief. We admire your courage. We admire your willingness to endure great pain upon the Earth, be it emotional, mental, physical, or spiritual. We admire you so very much, and we say to you today in NOW TIME, that the words "We love you" can never fully express the feelings that we feel for you. And so we embrace you now, ALL of you. All of you close your eyes and feel the vibrations of our Love, our deep, deep Love on this side of the Veil for ALL of you.

We wish you Peace. We wish you Love. We wish you happiness on your journeys forward. And for this day upon the Earth, this day of LOVE, of celebrating the memory of Valentine, the speaking is ended.

CHAPTER TWENTY-FIVE

MORE ON CORD-CUTTING;

A MEDITATION: JOURNEY THROUGH SPACE

We would say to begin today that it is good that you are making progress with the creation of both your website and the meditation we have given you to put upon a CD, which will allow you to offer it to those who would like to have a speaking of the meditation, and we say that the artistic imagery which will be coming to you will be most appropriate for this. This language that we are using is perfect for your purposes and for ours, for we are able to infuse these words with the vibrations of the Language of Light, and, as we have said, we will put those vibrations into the written words and onto the spoken words so that those who read and/or hear the messages we are giving to you will have a transformational experience even just by *holding* the CD or the book, and if there is another format that you will find, even in that.

We would like to say that we would urge you to take up the cord-cutting, as it will become very important in the near future that you will have cut as many cords as possible. We urge you to remember that before you come in contact with another being, that you repeat the phrase in whichever way you prefer: "No more cords to be attached" or "No attachment, no cords" — anything of that sort, and if you can phrase it in a positive manner, it would be even better. We leave that up to you to find the correct phrasing which feels good to you. (*The Co-author uses: "I am free of all cording from NOW forward in my life".*) Just know that it must be stated, and you may make one blanket statement if you like, to your Higher Self to prevent all establishment of cords between you and others. Prevent them all, for you do not wish to spend the rest of your days cutting cords that might be established from here forward. Remember, remember to make the statement and continue cutting the cords until you are certain that you have cut cords with everyone that you have come in contact with.

We say to you also that it is wise to cut cords with those from other lifetimes with whom you have not had contact in this lifetime on this Earth. This we recommend that you do in association with your Higher Self, with your Guides, and with us, and you would do it in this way:

"I call upon my Higher Self, I call upon my Guides, I call upon the Archangels now to bring before me any known or unknown beings with whom I have cords from other lifetimes, one by one, and we will cut the cords together. I ask you to help me because it is something that is kept hidden because of the Veil, and so I need your help, all of you, in order to cut the cords with individuals with whom I have cording, but whom I do not know, consciously, in this lifetime."

And in this way, you will be presented with the individuals or beings with whom you have cords and with whom you wish to cut the cords. And we remind you that we have said before, if you have cording to a being of extremely high vibrational frequency, it is not necessary to cut the cords with that individual, for that individual will be a teacher, a mentor, an Ascended Master, an Angel, a Guide, a Being with whom it is advantageous for you to remain in contact, and in close contact through the cord, which, generally speaking, will be through the heart. It could be from the crown chakra, but we do not see very many of those types of connections. It is quite seldom, quite unusual to be connected to another in that way, and you can rest assured that if you have a cord into your crown chakra, you need not remove it. And in fact, the removal of it could be quite disadvantageous for you. So we ask you to leave any cording that you might find, but it's not likely that you might find any in your seventh chakra. And leave all cording with those Beings with whom you have a close connection, such as Jesus, the Christ Light — we would not recommend to cut a cord with Him, — the Buddha, if you have a connection with the Buddha, any of the Ascended Masters, any of us, any higher Angelic Beings such as the Seraphim, and of course with The Creator — you are always connected to The Creator, and we will not elaborate on that.

❈❈❈

A MEDITATION: JOURNEY THROUGH SPACE

We ask you now to relax once again, take a deep breath, return to that deeply relaxed state that you recently left, and we ask you now to visualize a field of stars shining in the night sky. We wish you to feel the energies of the stars in the sky, and if you will come with us now, we will lift you up and take you with us to fly through the sky and feel the energies all around you. So if you are prepared now to leave your body behind and come with us, take another *deep*, relaxing breath ... and come with us now ... as we rise slowly up ... and travel ... beyond your Earth ... beyond the other planets ... beyond your star, the Sun ... and off into the darkness of space ... which is not empty, but filled with myriads of beings ... which are dark in color, but bright in their essence . . . they are here . . . to make the stars shine more brightly . . . they are magical beings . . . you would not be able to count them . . . there are so many of these beings . . . filling the spaces between the bright, shining stars and the planets surrounding them.

We ask you to come with us now as we zoom through the space which is not space, and remain aware that you can sense the vibrations of everything around you at all times. We wish to show you the wonders of the darkness and to allow you to discover that darkness is not frightening. The darkness is filled with warm, beautiful, magical beings who love you every bit as much as we do, and who welcome you now as you travel through their livingness. We know that this may seem very strange to you, but we ask you to suspend your disbelief and simply float and fly with us, fly with us through the spaces of the darkness and know that you are firmly connected to your body at all times. You need never fear the loss of your body, for we are with you, we protect you, we will return you to your bodies. Be not afraid.

And as we fly through the darkness, we occasionally see a star that perhaps pulls our attention, and we go closer to visit that star, that sun of another system, and we see the light as we come closer and closer to that star. Its light spreads out through the darkness, and if you are quick, in the area between the dark and the light, you might even be able to see the magical beings in the space between things, for when they are completely dark, you may only *feel* them, and when they are completely light, you may only *feel* them. But in the in-between space, if you are quick, you are able to see them, briefly, as a flash, and then they are gone again.

As you pass closer to the sun, and you feel the warmth of the rays of the star that is a sun, and you know that some of these stars are much larger than your Sun, and the ones that are really, really, really large would make it difficult for some beings to exist upon a planet that might be very far away from this sun and still receive the warmth. We wish you to know that there are many, many, many more suns than you could possibly count, many, many,

The Golden Essence Is YOU

many more galaxies than you will ever see, and that the beauty of The Creator's Creation goes on and on and on in this particular universe. And then, there are other universes, which we will not visit, as you need to remain within *your* universe in order to be able to return to your bodies and this three-dimensional Earth that you inhabit. But what we wish you to know and understand is that your Earth is very, very special and that the appreciation of this fact is not always evident to humans.

As we return now, back through the darkness, we will slow down our speedy return as we come closer to *your* Sun, and you may have what might be termed an "overview" of your Solar System. Look at it, for we are here now. Look at the beauty of it, the balance, the symmetry and the position of your beautiful planet Earth, exactly, perfectly in the place that is most advantageous for you to exist as humans in the third dimension and beyond. And we say to you that this journey we are taking you on is simply to let you know how wonderful this planet is and how beautiful it is, and we ask you to care for it in every way possible. Enjoy its features, enjoy its beauty: the waters, the forests, the mountains with snow, the tropical waters, the arctic waters. This planet is very special, VERY special indeed, and so many of you are not aware, and take it for granted.

We bring you back now, entering the atmosphere here very slowly, coming back to your various positions upon the Earth at this time, and we return you to your bodies. We ask you to remember everything you have seen, heard, experienced, and felt upon this journey out into what is called "space", but is actually *full*, and we ask you to honor the Earth by taking care of any space upon the Earth that you possibly can, in any way that you can think of, to honor and care for the Earth, your Mother, for the time that you live upon it in physical, human form or in, possibly, animal form. This may be a surprise for some of you, that you might possibly be an animal, but some of you have already existed as animals here upon the Earth, and some of you have other lifetime possibilities of existing as animals if you like. So we say to you today that you can become an Archangel to the Earth, and care for the Earth with the Love that we care for you, and with the Love that we carry for you, and with the Love that we stream forth for you now and always.

※※※

And for this day, the speaking is ended.

CHAPTER TWENTY-SIX

BREATHE IN THE SUN

We greet you this day, and we ask you to begin to imagine the Sun shining all around you. And we ask you to breathe deeply and to draw the light of the Sun into your bodies, and to continue with this visualization while we talk with you. Every time you take an in-breath, imagine that you are pulling the light, the energy, and the warmth of the Sun into all of your cells, for the Sun that you know in your Solar System is a part of All There Is and represents the Greater Sun, where The Source of All There Is dwells, and pulses out Its energy constantly to all of the other suns everywhere, all of the other creations everywhere, but most especially to the suns, and in particular, in your Solar System to your Sun, which pulses out its Light to sustain you, its energy and its warmth. Without your Sun, you could not exist upon this planet in the form in which you are existing now. Your life would be extremely different and not at all able to support you in the way in which you are now supported by the light, the warmth, and the energy coming from this what seems to you to be gigantic orb that you call The Sun, but which is very small in comparison to other orbs in the universe.

There are many, many other stars in this universe and elsewhere which are much, much larger than your Sun, but your Sun, and your Solar System, is the correct size for the sustenance of life upon the Earth, and everything is in its balance in the revolving around the Sun of the various planets, asteroids, comets, et cetera. We wish you to understand this, because the understanding of the position of the Sun is important for your comprehension of the Ascension Process, and when the Earth changes as she is changing now, it is important for you to understand that change is necessary for the Ascension Process. We do not wish to alarm you, but we do wish for you to see the larger view that *we* see from this side of the Veil.

We sense that our messenger is concerned about the source of this material *(the information was coming in very rapidly, and the rhythm of the speaking was not familiar)*, and we say in answer that we are those Beings of The Light spread throughout the universe who maintain the balance between the creations, some of which are not solid, but still have mass, and are basically considered creations no matter what, visible or not, tangible or not, and we wish you to know that there is a balance in the universe of which you yourself, or, in the many, you yourselves, are a part, and that you have your part to play in the transitional

The Golden Essence Is YOU

period which is upon you now where your planet is transforming itself with our help, with your help, with the blessing of All There Is, into a place of higher frequency than is now experienced by all of you. And in order for this higher frequency to manifest, there must be physical changes upon the Earth, which may be difficult for many of you to experience, or to witness, if you do not experience.

We have come today to help you understand about the changes, and about the experiences, and we ask you to remember to breathe *in* the Light, breathe *in* the Energies, breathe *in* the Warmth of that orb you call The Sun, and continue with breathing *in* these three substances, for they are very encouraging, they are very soothing to the human being, to the human body, and they will help you to feel the truth of what we are bringing through to you and for you. For the Ascension is, of necessity, a process of upheaval, a process of change, and you have *all* agreed before coming into human physical form that you will participate in this changing period of life as you know it upon your Earth.

We wish you to remember to remain steadfast, to remain secure, to maintain the feeling of safety around yourselves, and to know that if it is your Contract to remain upon the Earth during the changes, that you will do, and if it is not your Contract to remain upon the Earth, then you will find a way to come Home, and to observe with the rest of All There Is what will transpire upon your planet in the next years of Earth "time".

We wish those of you who choose to leave, to know now, ahead of time, that your transitions will be extremely beautiful and that you will be received with great rejoicing, as we know, for the human mind, it is difficult to understand and perceive what you have termed "death" or "dying", and these terms have, in your consciousness — in your what you call your collective consciousness — these terms have taken on an aura of fear for most, not for all, but for most.

It is difficult for many because of belief systems and teachings to understand that leaving your body behind and coming Home is a beautiful "re-birth process" in which you become free, freer than you have ever felt in your life upon the Earth with its gravity, free as you have only felt in the past, in your terms, in some of your dreaming states, or in your rememberings of leaving your body behind as it sleeps and journeying forth back to *here*, where we *all* are, we who have no human form, we who live as energy, we who exist in total freedom, total beauty, total creativity.

And so we wish you to know that you have nothing to fear but the concept of fear and the fear itself. Fear itself is the most fearful thing about what you call the "death" or "dying process" and if you know, as we know, that the return to this side of the Veil and the leaving behind of the physical form, which may or may not have been in great pain as you leave it, or great fear, leaving that all behind and becoming a Being of Light again is something that you all can look forward to with great anticipation and joy, and we wish that for all of you, for the apprehension and the fear, the negative aspects of these sensations, slow you down and cause your transition to be something different, not quite so enjoyable as the joyful anticipation of returning back to your origins, back to the Love that exists here, everywhere, back to The Source, if that is your intention. So we wish now to assure you, to reassure you, to hopefully give you comfort with our words.

If you are still breathing *in* the warmth, the energy, and the comfort of your Sun, you will begin to feel our words in your bodies, in your cells, in your flesh, in your bones, in your nerves, you will feel the truth, the absolute truth of the ***joy*** of returning Home when it is your time to return. And we wish you to know that those of you who have decided to stay with the Earth during her transition and your transition into Beings of Light upon the Earth, we have *so* much admiration for your choice, for your courage, for your sense of adventure, and your willingness to remain with the Earth on her journey through to Ascension.

We have no words for this, and if you will now take a moment to *feel,* we will send you those feelings that we have spoken of, so take a breath and feel the feelings we have for you... *(pause)*... and know that we love you, our Beings of Light in human form, with a Love that never ends and is deeper, fuller, and richer than any feelings you have ever felt in human form.

Begin to use your *feeling* senses more and more, for these will soon become more important to you than your thinking. Center yourselves into your hearts, and place every decision that you must make there, and not in your head or elsewhere. *FEEL* life now with your hearts. Begin to become accustomed, begin to become accustomed *now* to feeling instead of thinking, and knowing through the heart. The center of Love is the heart, and we wish you now to consider making the heart the center not only of your *love* but of all your communications. Breathe in now and feel the Love that is all around you in your air, in your Sun, in everything that you experience as beautiful and true.

And for this day, these are our *truths*, and we send them to you with all the Love that exists.

And for now, the speaking is ended.

CHAPTER TWENTY-SEVEN

AGREEMENTS MADE BEFORE "THE BEGINNING"

We are the Archangels this day and we greet you.

We would like to say to you that we urge all of you to remember who you are: That you are *all* — those of you who are hearing these words or reading them upon a page, or even on the Internet, those of you coming into contact with our speakings — it would be good for you *all* to remember, or to become acquainted with, the idea of this truth:

You are all beings of Eternal origin. You are all Beings of Light. You are all beings of high, high energy, and you are temporarily living upon the Earth in what is called a "physical form". This physical form has a beginning, a growing and birth into breathing the air of the Earth, and an ending, when the physical form becomes too weak to continue existing upon the Earth. It is at this point, which you call "death" and we call "rebirth", that you are reborn back to this side of the Veil, which is in place by consent of all who come to Earth, to keep you from "seeing" that which you have left behind and the magnificence and beauty of all that exists here where we are and where other Beings of Light, including The Creators, The Goddesses, The Gods, and of course, The Source of All There Is, The One Creator, where we all exist in our true forms of energy. If you stop now and *feel* the sensations in your bodies, attune your consciousness to *feeling* instead of *thinking,* and you may be able to feel the pulsing of your nervous system, the activity within your skin. This is something that is, in a small way, similar to what we feel on this side of the Veil: AN ENERGY FIELD OF LIGHT AND LOVE.

We wish you to understand this more than any other concept that we may have presented to you within the form of this book:

YOU ARE AND ALWAYS WILL BE.

YOU ARE ENERGY AND ALWAYS WILL BE.

YOU ARE LOVE AND ALWAYS WILL BE LOVE.

And your experiences upon the Earth which may not be of Love, which may be the opposite, totally, in which you may exist with a total *lack* of Love, in which some of you may not even understand what Love is, for you have never experienced it in physical form — these are all a part of the Agreement made between Souls before the creation of this planet and before the first Beings of Light appeared upon the planet, and they were not in physical form, but much later, when they decided to take on a denser aspect, they became closer to what you experience now as human form.

This all has been occurring because of an Agreement made before everything, that you would *all* experience all there is to experience upon a planet which is, more or less, solid, in bodies which are more or less solid and have experiences of all kinds. You all decided to give yourselves the freedom to choose, to create your lives as you wish them to be, and you all agreed to place what you have learned to call "the Veil" between here and where you are so that you would not all leap right out of your bodies and return Home at the first sign of trouble.

So most of you do not remember that you have come from a place which some might refer to as "Heaven", "Paradise". You have come from a place of extreme beauty, of harmony, of love, of cooperation, of creativity; there is NO THING negative on this side of existence. The negativity that many of you experience upon your planet is a creation of all of you and is recognized as a learning tool for all of you and most of you experience it at some point, in order to understand the striving for THE LIGHT, in order to understand the creations of the various religions upon your planet, in order to understand the yearning for GOD, the yearning for THE LIGHT.

Marilyn Zschau Baars

You yearn for it because in the deepest, deepest hidden parts of you there exists a point of Light in every one of you. And once you find it, you know the Peace of knowing that you are ETERNAL. But we say to you that those of you who are *not* aware of this Light within you have constantly searched for the Light outside of you, for you have been unable to discover the Light that you so deeply yearn for. And we say to you that once you close your eyes, and sit quietly, removing all thoughts, and just *feel, feel* for the sensation of Peace. Begin with PEACE. Begin with CALM, CALMNESS, QUIET, and just sit with the feeling of PEACE, CALM, and QUIET, and if you continue in this way, eventually, you will find the Light within yourselves. You will see that Eternal part of you in your mind's eye, and you most certainly will feel within your *heart* the stirrings of the feelings of deep Love, which is your birthright.

And so, we say to you that any method that you use to lead you to the "Inner Light" is good. If you choose to take a different path from the one we are suggesting, that is perfect for you. Any path, that ends with your feeling that YOU ARE LOVE, is good for you. Any path that leads you to feel unworthy of Love is not good for you, unless you wish to add it to your storehouse of knowledge.

We say to you now that our greatest and deepest desire is to be of service to you, and to help you when asked at all times. Remember to call upon us. We so eagerly await your call. Know that we are here for you, and that we will do *all* in our power to help you with anything that you need, even if it means changing your Contract to remove certain parts which may have caused you some pain, or at least, discomfort upon your journey in human form.

We add that we understand everything that you are experiencing upon the Earth, and that we know that there are many challenges ahead for most of you in the coming years of Earth time. We ask you to remember the Words and to remember to establish a platform or platforms of Words for yourselves every day. These vibrations of the Words will help you more than you know, through any sort of discomfort, physical, mental, emotional, or spiritual, that you might have. The Words, the Triad Platforms, are something that we would recommend that you immerse yourself into daily.

Perhaps you would choose a Triad of Words for an entire week of Earth time. Perhaps you would choose a Triad of Words for only one day. Perhaps you need to change your platforms hourly to help you through situations that might be difficult in some cases, at your workplaces, for example, or with your personal relationships, as another example. The Words can help you through any situation, and we gently urge you to use them to help yourselves, for of course you are capable and able of helping yourselves in all of your situations that you encounter upon the Earth in your daily living.

We offer our services at any time for any thing, no matter how small or how large, and if it is within the parameters of your Contract with your Soul, you will be given help. If you ask for help and it is *not* given, you may understand that there is possibly a concern between your Soul, your Guides, and your Higher Self as to the best course of action. In that case, you may consult with your Guides and your Higher Self directly, and if you *are* in contact with your Soul, by all means, you may contact your Soul for information, although we say that for most of you this is not possible at this time. But you may always call upon your Higher Self. Your Higher Self is always allowed to help you, to give you advice if you ask, and to consult with you about your Contract. There are many other ways to find out the details of your Contract, but we will not go into those here. You may search them out, if you wish. Sometimes they are much faster, in some cases.

We are the Archangels and many more, and we send you our Peace, now and always.

CHAPTER TWENTY-EIGHT

MEDITATION: THE BUBBLE OF GOLDEN LIGHT

We greet you this day, and we would like to say to begin that the conditions are perfect for communication. (MZB: *It was raining.*) You are becoming more and more open through the meditation ("The Journey to the Sea of Light and Love") and it is becoming much easier for us to send information through to you, which you can assimilate in a manner that can be then spoken.

We tell you now that you need not concern yourselves with the changes that are coming to the Earth over the next period of Earth time, that you are well equipped to continue with the Earth forward through the Ascension Process.

Marilyn Zschau Baars

We would say to those of you reading this material and/or listening to it in an audio format that the coming years of Earth time will be bringing many changes. You have already seen the beginnings of the changes. We ask you to become more flexible in your outlook, more flexible in your expectations, more welcoming to new ways of accomplishing things, and become accustomed to the idea of "letting go" — letting go of the old three-dimensional concepts of "right and wrong", "up and down", "left and right", "black and white", and begin to see all of the colors which are coming through, and we do not just mean physical colors with — seen with the eye — but colors of vibrational frequencies of new inventions. They are already coming in and are becoming manifest. We ask you to begin to *expect* changes in the way that things happen. There will be new inventions that will be surprising, and new ways of running things. This will all become gradually apparent over the next years. But we ask you all to be flexible. Know that you are protected. Know that you are safe. Know that all is unfolding according to your Life Plan, and look forward with great anticipation to the changes coming onto the Earth.

We ask you now to close your eyes once more and for those of you reading this, you may just continue to read, remaining in a calm, meditative mind-set, and you will be able to accompany the rest of us on this journey, for there is no Time, there is no Space, there is no difference, and any time that you close your eyes and entrain your vibrations with the vibrations of others, and with *us* and with All There Is, you are receiving whatever information may be given out in the *NOW*.

So close your eyes, take a deep, relaxing breath, know that you are SAFE, that you are SECURE, that you have WELL-BEING, and just listen as we lead you through another meditation, a meditation of calming peace and peaceful calm, a meditation which you may use over and over again and which will, with each use, bring you more and more into a state of peaceful calm, or calm peacefulness.

✷✷✷

MEDITATION:
THE BUBBLE OF GOLDEN LIGHT

So we ask you now to imagine yourselves just lying down peacefully, somewhere of your own choosing, in the most beautiful place that you can possibly imagine that you might like to just lie down and relax. It could be on the warm sand beside the shore of a beautiful sea, it could be upon the lush grass of a meadow filled with flowers, it could be anywhere that you like, even off of the planet Earth, if that is your choosing. You may return to *The Sea of Love* if you prefer. You may be in *The Field of Golden Essence*. In any case, imagine yourself lying down in the most beautiful place appropriate for you and just relaxing.

Imagine a golden ball of energy, of peace energy, of calm energy — a golden ball of energy enclosing you in its beauty, and you lie inside a bubble of gold, golden light, golden feelings, perfect peace and perfect calm. And within this bubble of golden light, you are always safe. Within the bubble of golden light, you are always protected. Within the bubble of golden light, you can communicate with all the other Beings of Light, if you wish. Know that this golden bubble of light is filled with LOVE for you, all for *you*. You may enter the bubble of golden light at any time you wish, simply to feel the love that exists there only for *you*. This is *your* bubble of perfection, of peace, of love and of light. And in your bubble of golden light, everything is perfect, everything is peaceful, everything is right and good and all of the wonderful words that you can possibly imagine, all of the words associated with perfection, with beauty, with light, with love, with peace, with calmness. All of the words are available to you that are soothing, loving, kind, respectful. Everything that you have ever desired of a positive nature is available to you within the golden bubble of light and love and peace and perfection.

And so we say to you now that this is, in a way, a mini space vehicle for you, for traveling safely wherever it is that you wish to be. The golden bubble of perfection is the place to go whenever you are feeling any feelings of a negative nature. If you are feeling fearful, take a deep breath and close your eyes and enter into your golden bubble of perfection. Just imagine it, feel it, sense it, see it and know that you are there. It is very simple. It is easy. It is very, very easy for all of you to imagine a golden bubble completely encasing you, your body and your entire energy field. Just pop into it and relax, relax, relax into the knowing that all that you wish for is within the Golden Bubble of Light and Love.

※※※

And now that you have experienced the bubble, we ask you to stay there as we continue speaking, for it is necessary, for some of you, to have an extra bit of Love and Light when we speak of events which may be a bit disturbing for some, and even if we mention the word "disturbing", we ask you just to breathe deeply and remain in your golden bubbles and know that you are safe, you are secure, you are at peace and you are love, love in the highest form possible upon the Earth at this time.

Love in this form, in the advanced form, is coming onto the Earth now, and the energies of this advanced form of Love, which is called "advanced" because it is of a higher vibrational frequency than the love you generally feel upon the Earth, this Love which is flowing onto the Earth now, and around the Earth, and into the Earth from the Creator Light — this Love energy can feel quite intense to those of you not accustomed to feeling such strong energies, and it may be confusing. It may cause some of you to become fearful. We say to you "Be not afraid", for this Love will raise you up. This Love will carry you forward. This Love will sustain you, and this Love will bring you more peace than you can possibly imagine is possible.

So, we ask you that when you begin to feel, in your normal day-to-day existence, a bit irritated, or even agitated, — a bit, possibly, uneasy —, we ask you to recognize these symptoms of the beginnings of feelings of fear, and to remember that it is all a higher vibration of the Love energy of the Creator Source of All There Is coming directly to you, through you, around you, through, around and into your planet, and it may feel very overwhelming to many of you.

We ask you, when you notice the first signs, to take a few moments, lie down if possible, relax, see yourselves in the most beautiful place that you can imagine, and enter into your golden bubble of love, perfection and light, and breathe slowly. The energies will be adjusted for you in your golden bubble and you will open up to the higher energies, or the faster energies, if you prefer. You will be able to open up to them within your golden bubble in a way that will allow you to absorb the energies without any feelings of negative emotions or fear.

The Golden Essence Is YOU

And we tell you now that it would be good to begin forming your golden bubbles by continuous repetition of this meditation, exercise, if you wish. Continue with this every day, even if you do not feel "pushed" by the energy, or even if you do not have feelings of irritation, of uneasiness, of feeling "strange" in your skin. Even without these feelings, it would be good to practice daily entering into your golden bubbles and relaxing for a few minutes. It does not need to take a long time, perhaps five minutes; ten minutes will be enough, even one minute, if you have the time, is good. Just see yourselves, feel yourselves, know yourselves and sense yourselves inside the golden bubble and take deep, relaxing breaths and know that you *are* a Being of Eternal Light, that you *are* in your very essence a creation of the Great Light. Know that you exist for ever, and that all that you could ever lose would be your human physical form, that you exist always and you *are* Beings of Light, temporarily encased in human form for a finite period of time. It has been so for a very long time upon the Earth, and what is coming will be bodies of LIGHT. Your human physical forms will transform themselves into LIGHT.

The more that you spend time in the *now*, practicing these exercises and meditations we have given you, and there are others, which have been developed by other Masters to help you through this coming period of "transition time" upon the Earth, you may choose to do visualizations and exercises given by others if you wish, and you may do our exercises and meditations that we are giving you *now*. We ask you most urgently to remain CALM and FEARLESS during the coming changes upon the Earth, and know that the more you see yourselves as a part of The Creator, the easier it *all* will be for you. BE NOT AFRAID, for THE GREAT LIGHT is coming onto the Earth, and the Earth herself is becoming a Being of Light. The Goddess Gaia has always been a Being of Light. What we are referring to is the physical planet EARTH, and that EARTH is becoming a BEING OF LIGHT as well.

We say to you now that in order for you to continue upon the Earth during this period as human beings, simply go about your business with a new awareness of who you are on this beautiful planet, and know who you truly are in your absolute Essence. Know that we are here as close as the skin upon your body to help you at all times, just ask. Ask for whatever it is that you need to know, that you need help with, just ask, and you will receive, if it is within your Life Plan or your Soul Contract it will be granted. We are here to help you. We are here for you, for we know that this is something very new for all of you, at least for this period in the history of the planet Earth it is new for you, and what is *spectacularly* new is that you have agreed to remain upon the Earth during her transition into LIGHT, and you have all agreed to transition into LIGHT as well, without dying, as you have known it in the past.

And now we ask you to open, open your hearts even wider as we send our deepest, most intense vibrations of Love into your hearts to give you solace and to soothe your pain.

We love you beyond measure and we *are* the Archangels, ready to assist at any moment. And for today, we say to you these are the truths of "What Is", and the speaking, for now, is ended.

CHAPTER TWENTY-NINE

ABSORBING THE INCOMING ENERGIES

<u>Note to Readers/Listeners</u>: I am including this personal message because I feel the information is important for you also.

The Archangels: We are here and we would ask you, to begin, to choose three words for your platform, which are appropriate for you for today.

MZB: "I choose CONFIDENT, CALM, and PEACEFUL."

"Frans chooses FREEDOM, PEACE, and FORGIVENESS, FORGIVING."

The Archangels: Very good. These are both platforms that are appropriate for you for this time in your development, and we would say further that you would do well to choose each day upon arising a platform to base your actions upon for that day. It is always good to establish these words as a habit practice, for these words will help you, as we have said, through the next periods of Earth time, and on into the Ascension Process, which is ongoing at this moment, but not particularly obvious to many.

Today, we would like to speak with you about the book, about the information, which also needs to be included. We are not quite ended with the messaging. We wish to bring through one more meditation, if you like, and we will do that soon.

For today, we wish to say to you that it would be good for you to relax more, worry less, and *feel* for the flow of energies every day. Become more accustomed to *feeling* the flow of the energies, which are coming onto the Earth now from The Source. The Creator Light is sending forth waves of energy to be absorbed by all who will, in order to transform yourselves into Beings of Light. If you can open up yourselves to accept the energies, and you may need to sit quietly, close your eyes, and *feel* rather than see or think. *Feel*, for example, NOW. What are you feeling? You are feeling, as we perceive it, slightly energized. Your bodies seem to be buzzing a bit. Is this so?

MZB: "Yes."

This is the way in which you absorb these energies:

> Sit quietly with your eyes closed. Allow the worries and thoughts and any other feelings to drop away. You may state an intention if you like,

such as "I wish now to feel the energies coming onto the Earth from The Source Creator of All There Is." And then, just *feel*, breathing in the energies through every pore in your body and breathing out, so the in-breath should be long and slow. Breathe the energies into every pore. Take another breath now. And we would ask you now, "Are you feeling any different on the in-breath?"

MZB: "Yes, I am. Frans also feels different. I see Light in my head. Frans, are you seeing Light? He feels it around his heart."

Very good. Both are valid responses to this energy, and we ask you to continue with this for another few moments. We will remain silent.

As you can see, and feel, the energies are both energizing and peaceful. All you need do to absorb the energies is give the intent, pay attention when you are breathing, allow for the feelings, and allow them to sink into your body to become integrated. In this way, you will facilitate the physical changes in the body, which are necessary to create the Crystalline Forms within the body, which are necessary for the Ascension Process, and for the changes within the body, which will be coming. So we would advise, if it is permitted to advise, (Yes), we would advise that you do this slow breathing IN of the waves of energies from The Source Creator Light at times during the day when you think of it, if and when you may feel a bit nervous, if and when you may feel a bit stressed, at any time in which you feel anything other than *Love*. Take the time to sit quietly and breathe, through every pore in your body. Breathe into your body the vibrations of *Love*, the energies of the wave from The Source Creator Light. Absorb them into your bodies.

At the end of your day, as you are preparing for sleep, you might want to say something to your body about the assimilation of the energies, and you might want to instruct your body to release any old energies, which are ready to leave your body, easily, harmlessly, and peacefully through the dream state, so that you will awaken in the morning refreshed and eager to continue with breathing IN the energies.

And we also say to you that it might be good for you, if you would like to do this, to take a few moments at the beginning of your day before you arise from your bed, or wherever it is that you are sleeping, — take a few moments to breathe IN the energies, for they will energize you for your day ahead and give you the peace and calmness that you require, along with the energy to complete your tasks for that particular day upon the Earth, remembering always to ask your body to assimilate easily and harmlessly all of the new energies being sent in to it from The Source Creator Light. And in this way, you will prepare yourself for the times ahead, which may be becoming more stressful during the Ascension Process. We do not say that they *will* be stressful, but they may be for some, more stressful than their usual daily waking existence has been up to this point.

And so we say to you, that we are welcoming all of you to the Higher Light, the Brighter Light, the Light of The Source

The Golden Essence Is YOU

Creator of All There Is, and that we are watching you with great interest, as are many, many, many other Beings on this side of the Veil and elsewhere.

You are the center of attention in this universe at this point in the development of this universe, and of your galaxy, and in particular, of your planet. You are the center of interest, and every Being who exists and who is aware of what is happening upon planet Earth is filled with interest, with anticipation, with joy, not all, but most are filled with joy; some are only curious. There are also some who are skeptical that you will succeed, but we say to you, that is not important, for we know that you will succeed, and we urge you on with the greatest Love that we can send. We join our Love with the Love that you are receiving from The Source, The Creator of All There Is, for we are, as you are, also part of The Creator Source of All There Is, and we all rejoice to see you and your Ascension Process.

So we say to you today, that the most important things that we wish to say have been said, about the breathing IN of the energy into and through every pore in your body, not just through your nose, mouth, and lungs, but to every cell, every pore, every part. Every tiny part of your body receives this extraordinary gift of Love to aid you in the process of developing your body in order to ascend *in the body*, for it is easy to ascend out of the body. You leave it behind and you ascend. That is the easy part, of course. It involves leaving the body.

But we say to you that you will ascend IN your body, and we wish you to know this, to feel this, to sense this so that you will anticipate the Ascension with great love, with great joy, with great expectations, with happiness, with a feeling of coming freedom that knows no bounds. And so we say to you today: Enjoy your lives, enjoy this process, enjoy even those what may be called "disasters" upon the Earth, of the hurricanes, the winds, the rains, the huge storms, the shakings of the Earth, enjoy these without fear, for it does not mean that Mother Earth will be destroyed. It means that she is shaking herself and cleansing herself and preparing herself for the same process that you are going through: The Ascension.

And so, in closing today, we ask you to take a moment to feel upon — no — to feel *with* your hearts our presence around you, surrounding you with our protective Light and infusing you with our courage. We are flowing our Love into you now, into your hearts, and we ask you to rejoice with us. Rejoice, for the Ascension is upon you, and you are doing so well.

And for this day, and always, we are the Archangels and many, many, many more, and we love you beyond this, beyond knowing, beyond Eternity. And so it is.

CHAPTER THIRTY

THE CLEANSING CELESTIAL LIGHT SHOWER

Note To Readers/Listeners: I am including this personal message because I feel the information is important for you also.

We greet you this day, and we congratulate you for joining with us again this day, and we look forward to communicating with you both every day from now forward, for the times are changing, as has been sung by some of your popular singing groups, and the Earth changes will be accelerating over the rest of this current year of 2010, calculated in Earth terms, of course.

We ask you to become more aware, every day, of your particular place in the universe, and to remember as best you can what it is that you have promised to accomplish during the Earth changes period, and how you have agreed to be of service to your fellow travelers during this time of their great need.

We ask you both to remember, first thing in the morning when you awaken, that you are an Emissary from the Archangels, and to carry this thought with you throughout your day, reminding yourselves from time to time, especially in moments of need, that the so-called "third-dimensional experience" is now beginning to include parts of the fourth dimension and the fifth dimension. Remind yourselves when you are feeling confused, agitated, worried, concerned, — whatever it is that you are feeling on the emotional level —, remind yourselves that you can clear this with a number of different methods you already are aware of.

It would be good to cleanse your auras every night before sleeping and every morning upon awakening, for if you allow yourselves to remain open during sleep, there are now many, many who would like to invade or to send thought-forms into your emotional and mental bodies, which may be incomprehensible to you, but which may result in a great deal of confusion about what is happening to you.

It is imperative, it is *imperative* that you now place the cleansing of your auric fields at the forefront of your minds, and that you begin to do this upon a regular basis so that it becomes second nature, so-to-speak, and that it is the thing that you do in the morning, similar to taking a shower to cleanse the physical body.

You may take a Golden Light Shower to cleanse the emotional body, the auric field, the mental body, the etheric double. Just

The Golden Essence Is YOU

see yourselves standing under a shower of Light coming from above. Imagine that it is The Great Creator, for indeed, it truly is, sending Its Love, Its energies of peace, purity, love, and protection directly to you in a single line of beautiful, sparkling Golden White Particles of Celestial Light.

This Light will cleanse your auric field, and as you breathe in, remind yourselves:

> "This Light is cleansing me completely.
> This Light is removing all negative thought forms.
> This Light is removing all negative emotions.
> This Light is making me whole again,
> and I call upon this Light to surround me
> and protect me during my *day/night
> upon the Earth, this *day/night,
> and I give thanks to The Creator Light
> Who sends His Love in an unending stream
> of beautiful Light particles directly to ME,
> as well as to all others who are open and willing to receive."

---

* Morning/Evening

And so, in this way, you may be certain that you are cleansed, every night and every morning, and at any other time in which you may feel confused, alone, worried — any of those negative emotions that may afflict you and which you would like gone from your field.

Marilyn Zschau Baars

Call upon us and upon The Creator to cleanse you, for without this Cleansing Light, you may become lost in the multitude of other energies coming onto the planet now and surrounding you — from other people, other humans, other non-humans, other beings, dark beings — you name it, it can affect you <u>if</u> you forget to cleanse yourself. It must be a daily occurrence now. There is no more, "Oh, I forgot, I'll do it tomorrow", for on your tomorrow, it will be more than <u>twice</u> as difficult to remove all the negative thought-forms which have accrued over a forty-eight-hour period.

Best is to cleanse twice daily, at least, and be aware, be always aware, that the need for cleansing increases as your energy rises from the density of the third dimension into and through the fourth dimension, into the fifth dimension and beyond. It is more and more important every day to cleanse everything, physically and energetically.

And if you are still holding on to cords, we gently remind you: Choose a certain number and cut them daily. It matters not how many you cut in one day, or how few, but we tell you that the more you feel that you can cut in one day, the better you will feel in yourself, as you have seen.

We say to you also that when you are in need of feeling loved, please remember to open your hearts as wide as you can, to call upon us, and upon The Creator Source of All There Is. Call upon us for Love. We are streaming it forth at all times, but if you do not call upon us, and you do not open your hearts, the love will simply stream past you and not into you, for we are not allowed to force an opening in your heart, or to push our love into you, as much as we might like to do that when we see your need.

And so we say to you today: Take care of your emotional bodies, take of your physical bodies, take care of your mental bodies, and indeed, of all that is <u>you</u>. There may be even other bodies that you are not yet aware of. We ask you that when you pull Love into your hearts, that you spread it out as far as it will go, and in this way, you will cleanse and nourish all of your bodies. And who knows? You may nourish everything around you as well, not the least, each other.

And so, we take our leave now, surrounding you with our gigantic Wings of Light. Feel the Love that we offer to you now, and if we see that you have opened your hearts more to us, we will fill you even more full with Light — the Light of Eternal Love — the Light of the Flame of The Creator, glowing inside you at this moment with a warmth that never dies and an energy which sustains forever.

And now, for this time, the speaking is ended, but the LOVE continues always.......always.......always........*(whispered)*

CHAPTER THIRTY-ONE

THE CONSCIOUS BREATHING PROJECT

We greet you as always with the deepest love that we can possibly send to you upon the Earth plane, and we ask that you open your hearts even wider to receive an extra infusion of Love and Energy this day, for we would like to continue with the material we have been giving you for The Book of the Ascension, and today we wish to speak of the process involved in achieving the deepest state of brain waves which is necessary.

The deepest state is necessary in order for you to hear everything it is that we wish to convey to you now, so we ask you to take a deep, deep breath now, and when you let the air out of your lungs, while deep breathing, we ask that you imagine that this outgoing carbon dioxide is feeding all of the plants, including those in the waters of your oceans and lakes and rivers, in order to regenerate them. They are in need of more of the purest form of carbon dioxide, and that comes from you and all of the creatures upon the Earth who breathe oxygen in and carbon dioxide out.

Your awareness of what your breath is doing becomes more and more important as that which you call the Ascension draws ever closer, for the plants are also ascending. The plants are also ascending in their own Ascension Process and they have need of the carbon dioxide in a — what shall we say? — in a more <u>directed</u> way, with the knowledge coming from you and others that these out-breaths all of you are making are directly intended for their use. And you can begin with the plants inside your house, breathing upon each of them daily, sending them the loving breath of life, *directed* carbon dioxide, and then to the plants in your garden, and surrounding your house, and then to all the plants in your neighborhood, and so on, until you are directly aware that every out-breath you breathe is meant for the Plant Kingdom around your planet. The awareness of this will increase the quality of the carbon dioxide traveling outward from you and into the plants for their nourishment, for their regeneration, and for their own Ascension Processes.

We ask you to become more aware of not only this, but also of everything that you do, asking yourselves, "Is what I am doing now beneficial for the Earth, for the peoples of Earth, for myself, and for those near to me?" If the answer is "No", you may want to reconsider doing that about which you have asked this question. We wish you to become aware of every tiny thought, every tiny action, every tiny word that you speak, and know that everything is aware of you — everything — not just those in your direct neighborhood, but everywhere upon your planet, and indeed, in your galaxy, and in this universe and others. YOU ARE IMPORTANT. Remember this always.

Every in-breath and every out-breath from every being in physical form has an impact upon every other being in physical form, and indeed, upon every thing that exists. So when you begin to allow your thoughts to wander, stop yourself and ask, "Is this thought beneficial for all there is? Are these thoughts constructive or destructive? Are these thoughts indeed necessary for the good of all?"

It is time now for you to become aware, more aware, of your place in the All There Is, and for you to begin to acknowledge that you are an important member of All There Is.

We ask you now to take another deep breath, fully aware of who you are, and your effect upon All There Is. Do you feel a difference between this breathing and the breathing that you breathed before becoming aware?

"Yes".

We know, we know that you do, and we humbly ask all of you, now, all of you who have just become aware, and those of you who were already aware, and those of you who are becoming aware right now, we ask you to honor yourselves for the beautiful service that you now do for The All There Is by breathing consciously, and know, know beyond any doubt that when you breathe <u>IN</u> the energies of The All There Is, and the beautiful, clearing, and cleansing oxygen created for you, we ask that you breathe <u>IN</u> consciously as well as <u>OUT</u>, and we assure you that your lives will now be very different from the life you were living a few moments ago, before you became aware and before we requested that you breathe consciously.

We ask you also to teach others about this breathing so that they will breathe consciously as well, and we ask you to ask those to whom you speak about this breathing to teach it to others, and so, this way of Conscious Breathing will begin to proliferate upon the Earth, and more and more of you will become more and more aware, not only of your place in The All There Is, but of the great gift that you now are able to give to all others who compose The All There Is. The repercussions of this method of breathing are greater than you could possibly understand or know at this point in what you call "time" upon the Earth, but we tell you that you, too, have already started a revolution in planetary life, and we wish to thank you for your willingness to proceed with this Conscious Breathing Project.

We ask you now to take these thoughts and apply them, not only to yourselves, but also to the manner in which you think about yourselves and about others. We ask you to remember who you are and to remember us at all times. We will close now and we will continue later with the meditation for The Book of the Ascension.

We are the Archangels and we send you our Love always, forever.

CHAPTER THIRTY-TWO

MEDITATION: IN THE BEGINNING...

To The Co-Creators:

We greet you this day, and we say to begin that you are well on the pathway to returning to the easy flow, which we had established in the beginning of the giving of the information about The Book, and we suggest that you continue to tune in this early, or even earlier in the day, as we have said, for this part of the day and the morning is much quieter all around you, and it facilitates the communication in an easier and more flowing manner than if you wait until later in the day, when everything becomes more hectic, more busy, less peaceful, less quiet, and we would say to you now that the final meditation for The Book is one of great beauty also. And we wait for you to reach an even deeper level *(of brain wave)*.

Now we ask you both to take a deep breath.

And as you allow the Conscious Breathing breath outward, remember the trees, remember the plants, remember their dependence upon you for their life, for without your carbon dioxide, there would be no life for plants upon this planet. They are here to supply you with oxygen, and in return, you supply them with carbon dioxide. This is the plan, and this is the way that the cycle was created.

In the beginning of life upon the Earth we all joined together to bring expertise, knowledge of previous creation abilities, and projects to bear upon the creation of this planet and the life upon it. You were with us then, in your Light Forms, both a part of separate teams of Beings fulfilling the Creator's wishes and creating, yourselves, those aspects, which were required. You have an intimate knowledge of creation, even though you may not remember it consciously, of course. This knowledge is stored deeply in your DNA, for there was need of a place in the physical form for you to hide this information, and in the DNA it was deemed to be the best solution.

There is a great amount of information stored within your bodies, not only within the physical body, but also within the etheric, the emotional, the mental, the physical, the spiritual, and the other bodies rippling outward from you like the light from a star. You shine with all of the knowledge, each one of you, that you have learned over the great what you would call

"Time" that you have existed, but we would refer to it as "The Great Beingness", separate from The Creator, and still ONE with the Creator, so that you have an individuality, but you are not alone, for you remain, always, an energetic part of The Creator's Energy. Each of you is on an energetic level exactly the same. It is only upon this planet where you assume human form, a more solid representation of who you are according to your parents, and there you achieve the individuality of the bodies of Earth, and that is how you receive a feeling of being separate from The Creator, when in actuality, you are *not* separate from the Creator. You are the same, albeit very much smaller, extremely smaller, for the vastness of the Creator is not comprehensible to the majority of humans. There are some who do have a grasp of what it could be like to be as large, as vast, as infinite as The Creator, but they are very few, for even the idea of beginning to imagine what it might be like is, in most cases, extremely frightening to the egos of all of you, who become afraid that they will disappear into the vastness and never know an individual thought again.

But we say to you, egos: This is not the case, for you are very, very important for your human. You are put in place to maintain the individuality for the great experiment of life upon Earth, and human life in particular, for you are there not only to protect, but also to learn, to learn how to become a Being of Light yourselves. And we say to you that you need not fear the final exit from the body in what you have called "Death" or "The Dying Process", for you go on into the Light as well as your human, who is a Being of Light, and you begin to learn what it means to live fully, glowing in the Light of The Creator, that great Source of all energy, all knowledge, the all-seeing, all-powerful, ORIGINAL LOVE. For without The Creator and Its love for all there is, you would not exist at all.

And so we ask you now to continue breathing deeply and to listen, carefully, to that which we will now tell you.

✼✼✼

MEDITATION: IN THE BEGINNING...

Once upon a time, In The Beginning was The Energy and The Energy lives forever. And The Energy expanded, and suddenly became LIGHT, a Light so beautiful, so wondrous, so amazing that The Energy began thinking about what to do with The Light. And The Energy of The Source, The Light of All There Is, decided to create. And It began The Creation Process, which allowed It to take particles of Itself and create a separate Being of Light, the size according to the desire. And the separate Beings of Light were given permission to recreate themselves, over and over, and there was a ripple effect as the individualized

The Golden Essence Is YOU

Beings created by The Original Source began creating, themselves. And then, everything began to come into modified forms, and the modifications continued, on and on and on, endlessly.

There was some mutation which occurred, and that we will not speak of, for we wish you to concentrate your attention upon The Energy of The Light, The All-Seeing, All-Knowing, All-Hearing, All-Aware LIGHT of The Love of The Creator spreading forth from what you might term "The Heart of God, Goddess, All There Is" to all of Its creations, and continuing THE LOVE in a concentrated form, and infusing it into all of Its Creations, so that every thing, every being, every particle created is LOVE.

We wish you to understand this in the deepest parts of your beings, for a lack of understanding about BEING LOVE has given rise to many disappointments, misunderstandings, conflicts, wars, even, most especially upon planets where the beings have become "lost" and have become more and more warlike, forgetting in the process that basically, they are Love. They have taken on an armor of fear, distrust, greed, all of the negative aspects of life, for you live in duality where you are, and all is allowed, and so it is that you have what you term "Good" and "Evil". We would prefer that you call this "Light" and "Dark", for within the darkness still burns The Light of Love, however deeply suppressed, and in The Light exists, of course, the possibility of becoming Dark.

Those of you who struggle with being or feeling "Darkness" and a difficulty in feeling "Light and Lightness" must know that it is a matter only of choice. If and when you begin to feel negative feelings, sit quietly and remember what we say:

Choose to remember The Light within you. Choose to express The Light within you. And the more you decide FOR The Light, the more Light you will have within you, and the more Light that you have within you, the lighter you will become. And the lighter you become, the closer you are to transcending The Density and The Duality of where you are living, and have lived for so many eons of time upon the Earth.

The Golden Essence Is YOU

You have the choice to transcend the Darkness of Earth, and choose the Lightness of Love.

And so, we offer you now the choice of Light, the choice of Love, the choice of growth forward and outward, away from Darkness, away from negativity.

We offer you the opportunity to become that which you were in The Beginning: The most beautiful manifestations of The Beauty of Love as created by The Source of All There Is In The Beginning.

We ask you now to remember. Remember and feel.

Open your hearts wider now and feel the infusion of The Creator's Love that we have been honored with transmitting to you NOW. Breathe it in as you breathe in the oxygen from the plants, and breathe it out to ALL around you. And keep breathing IN the Light of Love of The Creator. And when you breathe it out, consciously, be aware of spreading The LOVE of The Creator around you.

Breathe IN from The Source, and OUT to The World — IN from The Source and OUT to The World.

And in this way, you will create again The Beauty and The Love of The Original Earth.

Where ALL was PEACE, there will be PEACE again.

Where ALL was LIGHT, let there be LIGHT again.

And where ALL was LOVE, spread LOVE around you again.

Create with Us, create again with The Source, and know The Peace, The Understanding, The Commitment, and The Joy of loving and being loved in return by Us, by The Creators, and most especially, by The Source of All There Is.

❈❈❈

And so we wish for you to remain with these thoughts, these feelings, these sensations of LOVE as we take our leave now.

CHAPTER THIRTY-THREE

ADDITIONAL IMPORTANT INFORMATION ABOUT CORD-CUTTING

We are here with you as we have said, always, and we greet you this day, and say to you that we are happy to hear you using The Invocation, for as you have sensed, it becomes more and more important now to make certain that only those Beings of the Highest Love and Light are welcome.

We wish to point out to you that the most important aspect of these words that we are speaking, and the words that we have spoken, is that they be heard by others and that they be seen in written form, so that all may be able to become acquainted with the knowledge and begin their process, their processes, of beginning to change the way in which they feel and think and sense and grow by filling themselves with The Light of The Source.

Those who are in need of this information will be drawn to become acquainted with it, and those who are not interested — you may know that they have chosen their own path, and that is good for them.

We feel that you perhaps have enough information at this point to begin the process of editing yourself those words we have given you, making corrections, filling in the blank spaces, organizing the Index, and deciding upon chapter headings, if you wish them. You may use numbers if you wish. We leave the rest of this to you, for this is a co-creation between those of us here, and you.

We will say that we find the title you have chosen to be interesting. You may call the book anything that you wish. What you call it is not important. That it is available for a wide audience is all that is important. And so we ask you now to continue with the process of finishing the chapters so that they are in a form acceptable to a printer, and also to arrange for the meditations to be available in a format for those who want them, to hear. We leave it up to you, but know that we are here for the asking at any time that you may wish to have a confirmation, or ask for help, if you need help, in making corrections.

We say to you now that you have all of the information that we find important for inhabitants of your planet to hear, to know, to become aware of.

The Golden Essence Is YOU

We do not wish to make any predictions of future events because the future is nebulous, and, as you know from what we have given you, all that is truly available to you is NOW. In the NOW there is only NOW, there is only what is happening NOW, there is only the Conscious Breathing that you are doing. There is only the thought that comes about NOW.

We urge you to remain as much as possible in the NOW. The only time that we wish you to take a look at the "past" is when you are cutting the cords, for in these cases, you must remember who it is that you have cords with; but we ask you to make your stay in the "past" brief, — only long enough to write the name down and then return to the NOW to cut the cords.

Always cut the cords in the NOW TIME, not in the "past", but RIGHT NOW. Remember: It is important to cut cords in the NOW. You may change events in your "past" through hypnotic regression and rearranging the events, but you must cut cords in the NOW.

Do not attempt to go back into the "past" in your mind and cut the cords *there*, for the cord-cutting will only be effective *there*, and will not be effective where you are NOW, which is a different place, for in the "past" you were in a different place, were you not? And NOW you are in a NOW place. So remember: Cord-cutting only in the NOW.

We ask you now to continue with your editing, with listening to the messages you have recorded, with preparing your messages for re-recording, if necessary, certainly the meditations, and to make the small corrections and arrange the words so that you may proceed with getting this work published.

It matters not very much the outside of the book; it is what is <u>inside</u> that is important. You decide the size, you decide the print, you decide the format — <u>we</u> will infuse it all with our energies and the energies of The Source of All There Is. You may rest assured, we will take care of that energetic aspect, if you will take care of the third- and fourth-dimensional form.

We leave you now so that you may continue with our glorious work, and we say to you that we love you, both, beyond measure. And we wish for you both immeasurable success.

And we say today and always:

WE ARE THE ARCHANGELS.

WE BLESS YOU. WE LOVE YOU.

AND WE SEND YOU OUR LIGHT,

NOW AND ALWAYS.

AND SO IT IS.

APPENDICES

1. THE AFFIRMATIONS FOR THE JOURNEY TO THE SEA OF LOVE AND LIGHT

2. AFFIRMATIONS FROM THIS BOOK

3. THE CORD-CUTTING PROCESS

4. THE CLEANSING CELESTIAL LIGHT SHOWER

THE AFFIRMATIONS FOR THE JOURNEY TO THE SEA OF LOVE AND LIGHT

I AM THE HIGHEST FREQUENCY OF LOVE AND LIGHT.

I AM ONE WITH THE SOURCE OF ALL THERE IS.

I AM PEACE.

I AM LOVE.

I AM THE DIVINE CREATOR.

AFFIRMATIONS FROM THIS BOOK

MY HEART SPEAKS TO MY CELLS IN LOVE.

I LOVE MYSELF.

I LOVE MY CELLS.

I AM DOING WELL.

I AM DOING THE BEST THAT I CAN DO.

I AM HEALTHY.

I AM A POSITIVE BEING OF LOVE.

MY PSYCHE IS HEALTHY.

MY BODY IS HEALTHY.

I AM HAPPY.

I AM TAKING CARE OF MYSELF WITH LOVE.

I AM IN CHARGE OF MYSELF.

I AM IN CHARGE OF MY CELLS.

I AM IN CHARGE OF MY LIFE.

I EAT THE OPTIMAL FOODS FOR MY BODY.

I AM IN CHARGE OF MY EXERCISING.

I BREATHE FRESH AIR CONSCIOUSLY.

MY VIBRATIONS ARE HIGHER AND HIGHER EVERY DAY.

I AM LIGHT.

I AM LOVE.

I AM BEAUTY.

I THINK HEALTHY THOUGHTS.

I LOVE.

I AM LOVED.

I FEEL MORE AND MORE LOVE EVERY DAY.

I AM THE SOURCE OF ALL THERE IS.

I AM LOVE.

I AM LIGHT.

I AM A GREAT BEING OF LIGHT AND LOVE.

THE CORD-CUTTING PROCESS

*** THE INTENTION TO REMOVE THE CORDS MUST BE IN PLACE.

*** YOU MUST DESIRE TO STOP CONNECTIONS ON LEVELS THAT ARE DRAINING YOU.

1. Express the desire to sever the cording, return the energies of the other to them, and pull back into yourself your energies.

2. Sit in a quiet place where you are not disturbed.

3. Visualize the other person; see them standing before you NOW.

4. Speak to them to ask permission to release the cords.

5. If you get a Negative Response:

    a. Move to the Higher Self level of both.

    b. Ask your Higher Self to receive permission from the Higher Self of the other to cut the connections.

    c. When you have received permission from the Higher Self, convey this to the other person.

Say: "I have received permission from your Higher Self to sever these cords."

    d. They MUST agree if the Higher Self has agreed.

6. Take either your physical arm and hand, or an imaginary arm and hand, and imagine that you have either a scissors or a knife, a very sharp knife. You may make these GOLDEN in color.

7. Sever the cords in a rapid movement, and say:

"I now release your energies back to you, and I bring my own energies back to myself. I wish you well, and send you Light, Love, and Peace."

8. See your own cut cord in front of you and bring that energy back into yourself.

9. Pull that cord out from your body and dispose of it, in a downward motion, because the origin of a cord from someone else still contains a small particle of their energy. You do not wish to bring that energy into your body.

10. In the case of a cord, or cords, that YOU have sent into someone else:

Follow all procedures as shown above, until Step 6. At that point, reach out and <u>pull</u> your cord or cords away, gently, from the other person, allowing their energy to exit the cord as you pull it closer to yourself.

11. SEE their energy flowing out of the cord, back into them.

12. Wait until ALL of the energy is gone, then reach up and pull the other end of that cord out of yourself. Wrap it into a golden ball and give it to Mother Earth.

NB: THE PROCESS OF CORD REMOVAL AND CORD-CUTTING IS EXTREMELY IMPORTANT FOR THE ASCENSION, FOR IF YOU DO NOT RELEASE ALL THE CORDS, AND CALL ALL YOUR OWN ENERGY BACK INTO YOU, IT WILL NOT BE POSSIBLE FOR YOU TO ASCEND.

THE CORD-CUTTING PROCESS SHOULD BE UNDERTAKEN IN **NOW TIME**, NOT IN THE PAST!

IN THE CASE OF CUTTING CORDS WITH BEINGS NOT CURRENTLY IN HUMAN FORM UPON THE EARTH, SAY:

> "I call upon my Higher Self, I call upon my Guides, I call upon the Archangels now to bring before me any known or unknown beings, with whom I have cords from other lifetimes, and we will cut the cords together. I ask you to help me because it is something that is kept hidden because of the Veil, and so I need your help, all of you, in order to cut the cords with individuals with whom I have cording, but whom I do not know, consciously, in this lifetime."

THE CLEANSING CELESTIAL LIGHT SHOWER

"I CALL UPON THE ARCHANGELS TO BRING THE GOLDEN WHITE LIGHT OF THE SOURCE OF ALL THERE IS TO SHOWER DOWN UPON ME".

"This Light is cleansing me completely.
This Light is removing all negative thought-forms.
This Light is removing all negative emotions.
This Light is making me whole again, and
I call upon this Light to surround me and
protect me during my day/night* upon the
Earth, this day/night*, and I give thanks to
The Creator Light Who sends His Love
in an unending stream of beautiful Light
particles directly to ME, as well as to all
others who are open and willing to receive."

---

* Morning/Evening

RESOURCES

Ron Scolastico, Ph.D.: Transpersonal Psychologist
www.ronscolastico.com
rs@ronscolastico.com
P.O. Box 6556
Woodland Hills, CA 91365 USA
1-818-224-4488

Susan Scolastico, C.H.T
www.metaphysicalcounseling.com
P.O. Box 6556
Woodland Hills, CA 91365 USA
1-818-224-4488

Mary Goslen, Reiki Master Teacher, Usui-Hayashi-Takata-Fran Brown-Mary Goslen Lineage of the Usui-Satori System of Natural Healing:
Reiki School International
http://www.linkedin.com/pub/mary-goslen/13/724/353
marygoslen@bellsouth.net
1969 Hinshaw Avenue
Winston-Salem, NC 27104 USA
1-336-723-8788

Steve Rother, Channel for The Group
www.lightworker.com
1-702-871-3317
Fax: 1-702-396-3316

Lee Carroll, Channel for KRYON
www.kryon.com
The Kryon Publishing Office
1155 Camino Del Mar, #422
Del Mar, CA 92014 USA
1-858-792-2990
Fax: 1-858-759-2499

Kahu Fred Sterling, Medium for KIRAEL
www.kirael.com
Honolulu Church of Light
3075 Kalihi Street, Suite 101
Honolulu, HI 96819 USA
1-800-390-1886 Toll-free in USA only
1-808-952-0880 Office

Patti "Athenna" Sterling
www.silverwingsoflight.com

Joan Pancoe: Trance Channel, Karmic Astrologer, Psychic Therapist
www.joanpancoe.com
joanpancoe@aol.com
1-212-982-6820

Debbi Kempton-Smith: Astrologer
www.debbikemptonsmith.com
stargazer@debbikemptonsmith.com
P.O. Box 1801
F.D.R. Station
New York, N.Y. 10150 USA
1-212-750-0188

Jay Farnsworth: Teacher, HUNA & Subjective Communication
914 Gillespie Drive
Apartment # 44
Spring Valley, CA 91977 USA

Eric Pearl: The Reconnection and Reconnective Healing
www.thereconnection.com
info@TheReconnection.com
The Reconnection, LLC
P.O. Box 3600
Hollywood, CA 90078 USA
1-888-374-2732 Toll-free in USA only
1-323-960-0012 Office

Larry Valmore: PSYCH-K Teacher
www.sacredmind.net
Larryv@psych-k.com
8577 W. Hampden Avenue, #305
Lakewood, CO 80227 USA
1-303-984-2056

Richard Gordon, Originator, Quantum Touch
www.quantumtouch.com
P.O. Box 1240
Kapaa, HI 96746 USA
1-888-424-0047 Toll-free, USA only
1-808-823-0400 International
1-808-823-0445 Fax

Alain Herriot, Teacher, Advanced Quantum Touch
www.quantumtouch.com

David Quigley, C.C.H.T.
www.alchemyinstitute.com
info@alchemyinstitute.com
The Alchemy Institute of Healing Arts
567-A Summerfield Road
Santa Rosa, CA 95405 USA
1-800-950-4984 Toll-free, USA only

Marilyn Gordon, C.C.H.T.
www.hypnotherapycenter.com
mgordon@hypnotherapycenter.com
Center for Hypnotherapy
P.O. Box 10795
Oakland, CA 94610 USA
1-800-398-0034 Toll-free, USA only
1-510-839-4800

Susan Mokelke, Executive Director, The Foundation for Shamanic Studies; Shaman
www.shamanism.org/fssinfo/mokelke.html
www.heartandsoulsongs.com/
The Foundation for Shamanic Studies
P.O. Box 1939
Mill Valley, CA 94942 USA
1-415-897-4583 Fax

Surja Jessup, M.S./C.H.T.
www.surja.com
Body/Mind Transformation
2084 Blake Street, #6B
Berkeley, CA 94704 USA
1-510-848-7519

Henning and Mariana Linde
Universal Field Coaching
www.uf-coaching.nl
Soul & Art
www.soulandart.com
011-31-61-507-7551 (from the USA to The Netherlands)

Melainah Yee
www.sunlightonwater.com
www.familyofthedolphins.org
P.O. Box 4729
Kailua-Kona, HI 96745
1-808-896-2480
1-808-325-7742 Fax

Ronna Herman, Channel for Archangel Michael

www.ronnastar.com
ronnastar@earthlink.net
6005 Clear Creek Drive
Reno, NV 89502 USA
1-775-856-3654

James Tyberonn, Channel for Archangel Metatron

www.earth-keeper.net
22 Meadowridge Place
The Woodlands, TX 77381 USA
1-936-522-8804

Jim Self: Teacher, Mastering Alchemy

www.masteringalchemy.com
hello@masteringalchemy.com
302 West Crestline Drive
Boise, ID 83702 USA
1-208-297-5785

GLOSSARY

Affirmations: Affirmations are phrases, usually short, repeated aloud in order to impress upon the subconscious mind and the conscious mind a new concept that the human being wishes to embody, such as "I am healthy."

Akasha, Akashic Records: "Akasha" is a Sanscrit word for "sky" or "space"; the Akashic Records contain, according to some sources, all of the information about souls, both individually and in groups. This information can be accessed by especially gifted "seers" or "psychics" trained to access the Akashic Records.

Aliens: The term currently in use to define beings from another planetary or star system; beings not of Earth origin.

Alpha, Beta, Theta, Delta Frequencies: These are the most commonly referred to brain waves in the cerebral cortex and can be measured with an electroencephalogram; alpha waves occur within the frequency range of 8-12 hertz, theta waves occur within the frequency range of 4-8 hertz, and delta waves occur within the frequency range of 1-4 hertz. Alpha correlates to the awake but relaxed state of mind experienced in light meditation, theta waves occur during deeply relaxed states, such as during deep meditation, hypnosis, and pre-sleep, and delta waves occur in deep and dreamless sleep. The beta brain wave is the term for the fully awake, conscious human being, and is experienced at 12-30 hertz.

Angelic Beings: These are those celestial Beings of Light who are considered intermediaries between Heaven and Earth by members of the following religions: Judaism, Islam, Christianity, and Zoroastrianism. They manifest the qualities of love, peace, purity, and healing, among other of the so-called "beneficial" qualities.

Ascended Masters: A term for those human beings who became, through intensive training and study, enlightened through a process of spiritual transformation, and subsequently, after death of the body, became members of the Cosmic Council of Light, formerly known as "the Great White Brotherhood"; the term was first introduced by Theosophists in 1934 (see "Unveiled Mysteries" by Guy Ballard).

Ascension, The Ascension Process: To rise up, to ascend to a higher plane of existence, to leave the third dimension for another.

Aura, Auric Field: That energetic and luminous part surrounding the bodies of human beings, not usually visible to the naked eye, but which can be seen by other humans trained to do so; the field is a fluctuating, swirling mass of colors which some people relate to the emotional state of the human exhibiting the colors.

Avatar: This term is generally understood to apply to a Celestial Being or God, incarnated upon the Earth in a human form. "From the Sanskrit *avatara* – a going down, from *avatarati* – he descends, from *ava* – down + *tarati* – he passes over": Collins English Dictionary – Complete & Unabridged 10th Edition 2009 — William Collins Sons & Co. Ltd. 1979, 1986 — HarperCollins Publisher 1998, 2000, 2003, 2005 2006, 2007, 2009

Being: In metaphysics, a term generally used to define those celestial energies or essences that constitute a part of God, or The Source of All There Is, such as the Archangels, the Ascended Masters, and others.

Belief Systems: A particular set of views or opinions accepted as truth, but which may not be true, unless absolutely proven to be so. Many humans hold belief systems that deny the existence of a "Higher Power", for example, and they may be referred to by some as "atheists".

Brain Wave Frequencies: Please see "Alpha, Beta, Theta, Delta Frequencies".

Chakra, Chakras: In Sanskrit: "Wheel, circle". There are seven chakras in the human energy field, spinning either clockwise or counterclockwise. The emotions experienced and expressed by the human being are reflected in the chakras, thereby influencing the experiences of life on Earth.

Cherubim: Those angelic beings of a very, very high energy, second only to Seraphim in the Order of Angels, according to some religions.

Collective Consciousness: A term referring to the concept of shared experiences by all beings on Earth.

Contract with the Soul: Every Soul makes a Contract for itself before extending a portion of its energy into a human for a lifetime. Contracts with the Soul contain agreements for experiences that may be deemed valuable for the Soul to have in its storehouse of knowledge.

Cords, Grounding: A Grounding Cord is a tool used by a human to connect securely to the Earth, thereby "grounding" itself. It can also be used to empty all negativity from the human form and its energy bodies by mentally visualizing and releasing the negative energies down the Grounding Cord to Mother Earth. It is created mentally, usually by sitting in a still position, and by imagining a connection from the base of the spine to the center of Mother Earth. As the cord reaches the center of the Earth, it is usually secured in some manner to keep it connected there. One can imagine a hook, tentacles, a large stone, or a connection to a crystal at the center in order to keep the cord connected to the Earth. The cord can be small or very large, depending on the desire of the human creating it. When the cord is connected, the human usually feels "grounded", that is, more firmly attached to the Earth and to reality as he or she experiences that.

Cords of Attachment: These cords are energetic connections between two human beings. They carry emotional energy back and forth between humans and can be either positive or negative. They remain forever, if they are not consciously cut.

One can ask for the help of Archangel Michael in the cutting of Cords of Attachment.

Council of Light, The: A group of wise souls residing on the other side of the Veil; includes the Ascended Masters, among others. These souls are teachers, masters, and guides. Also known as "the Cosmic Council of Light".

Counselors: These are Beings on the Other Side of the Veil who assist souls in making decisions about soul growth and Life Plans.

Creator Gods, The: These are the "local" Creators of our galaxy; they reside in The Great Central Sun of our galaxy, the Milky Way.

Creator Source of All There Is, The: The Supreme Creator of everything that exists.

Devas: The word "deva" is from the Sanskrit, meaning, "shining one", and devas are shining, or luminous, beings who care for the Nature Kingdom of Earth.

Dimensions: There are generally considered to be ten to twelve dimensions. We currently live in the third/fourth dimension, and to "ascend" to the fifth dimension, where Unity Consciousness begins, we need to speed up our vibrational frequencies, as described by the Archangels in this book. For more information on the dimensions, I suggest this weblog: http://blogs.sun.com/bblfish/entry/the_10_dimensions_of_reality

Earth Changes, The: This phrase refers to the physical changes Mother Earth is currently experiencing, such as earthquakes, volcanic eruptions, floods, et cetera; everything of a physical nature that undergoes a change upon the Earth.

Elemental Beings: These beings are on Earth to care for the Nature Kingdom and all within it. They include devas, fairies, pixies, gnomes, elves, mermaids, and sylphs, among many others.

Energy Field: The human energy field is also known as the aura; see "Aura, Auric Field".

Etheric, The: A term from Theosophy, understood to refer to the energy of a human being, invisible to the eye, but visible to the advanced student of metaphysics. It completely surrounds the human body and replicates the body in energy.

Fairies: see "Elemental Beings".

Framing: Giving a subject a possible different meaning by positing several frames of reference that might suggest a different perspective. Also, changing a negative phrase or statement so that it becomes a positive phrase or statement.

Free Will: On the Earth, we have been given the gift of Free Will by The Creator Source of All There Is. This means that we all have the ability to choose whatever we wish to choose, individually, in our lives as our courses of action. This is not necessarily true on other planetary systems in this universe.

Gaia: The name of the Earth Goddess. (ORIGIN: From the Greek "Gaia", meaning "Earth".)

Gnomes: See "Elemental Beings".

Guides: Guides are spiritual beings, not incarnate on the Earth, who help humans in making choices in life. Sometimes called "Guardian Angels" or "Spirit Guides".

Higher Self: A term that refers to that spiritual part of the human that is in contact with the Higher Realms and with The Creator Source of All There Is. It is a Golden Being who can be found in the heart, and can be consulted on any questions that the human may have.

Language of Light, The: The language of communication on the other side of the Veil; the Universal Language. Some human beings have the gift of being able to speak this Language of Light and Love.

Life Plan: A term referring to the decisions made before incarnating into a human body upon Earth; the pre-incarnation goals and experiences desired to be played out in the "human drama". See also: "**Contract with the Soul**".

Life Review: The process that the Soul Part of a human enters into after death of the physical body and re-birth into the true "Home" of the Soul. The Life Review is undertaken with one's Guides, Counselors, Master Teachers, and other Beings of the Light, and may include Angels. It is a complete review of the entire lifetime just finished, and consists of determining whether or not the goals decided upon before incarnating have been achieved, and which goals will be either repeated or left for another incarnation. If a Soul has achieved the highest level of experience and wisdom available to it in its lifetimes, it might cease to incarnate and become a Guide to souls still in the incarnation process.

Mantra: A mantra is one word or a series of words that may be repeated over and over again to quiet the mind during meditation, and can be considered a transformational tool. "Om mani padme hum" is an example. "God is Love" is another example.

Other Side, The: A term that refers to the "place" that is on the other side of the Veil; where Soul Parts go after death of the physical body; also known as "Heaven", "Paradise", "Home".

Past Lives: Lifetimes or incarnations previous to the current one that have been experienced by the Soul, and that can be "remembered" through various techniques, especially during hypnosis. These are sometimes referred to as "Other Lives" rather than "Past Lives", as all "time" is simultaneous, according to the Archangels.

Psychics: A person who is able to "see" beyond the physical, and also "hear" beings from beyond the Veil.

Regression Therapy: The process, usually hypnosis, of retrieving memories of "Past Lives" or "Other Lives".

Seers: Those humans who have the gift of "seeing" that which is hidden from the "normal" human; also referred to as "Psychics".

Seraphim: The highest of the High Angelic Beings in The Order of Angels, and closest to The Creator Source of All There Is, according to beliefs held by various religious groups.

Sixth Sense: A term referring to that ability possessed by all, but recognized by few, that gives one ESP (extrasensory perception) to sense information not readily available to the other five senses.

Soul Contract: See "Contract with the Soul".

Soul Essence: The innermost, most important, and most crucial aspect of a Soul; that which delineates a Soul and separates it from another; the essential part of a Soul.

Soul Group: Souls that are all members of a specific group, perhaps since their creation, and containing teachers who may or may not act as personal spirit guides to members in their group.

Soul Part: That part of the Soul that incarnates onto the Earth.

Transformational Experience: A super-normal experience that causes a reaction, transforming the human being who has the experience. In the Christian religion, Saul/St. Paul had a "transformational experience" on the road to Damascus.

Universal Law: The universal agreement entered into by ALL souls everywhere; for example, no one is allowed to interfere in another's development without their explicit invitation to do so.

Veil, The: The term that refers to that "forgetting" of what one has left behind when incarnating into a human body upon the Earth. Almost all souls agree before incarnating to place "the Veil" over their consciousnesses so that they will be able to remain upon the Earth for a specific length of time. It is generally agreed that if "the Veil" were not in place, no one would come to Earth, but would remain in "Heaven", "Paradise", or "Home", which is on the other side of "the Veil".

Vibrational Frequency, Vibrational Level: The energy of the human body vibrates at varying rates, depending on the development of the energies within that body.

"Wake Up": A phrase referring to a suggestion by the Archangels for the humans who are still unaware of their essences, which is that they are ALL Great Beings of Light and Love. A very large group of humans on this planet are considered to still be "asleep", and are unaware of their True Essences.

"What Is": A term referring to the actuality of the generally agreed-upon basic truths of existence for all beings, celestial and/or human.

ABOUT THE AUTHORS

"And know that we are who we say we are: WE ARE THE ARCHANGELS, ALL, and many more, unnamed, but truly existing. There are innumerable ones of us, and this may be difficult for many to believe because of the limitations placed by religious groups upon the naming and the numbering of so-called 'Archangels', but we assure you there are many, many, many more than anyone could ever count. We are Infinite and we are in a sense, One." ---The Archangels, from their book "THE GOLDEN ESSENCE IS YOU".

The Archangels have been communicating with Marilyn Zschau Baars for over 25 years, but it has been only since 2003 that she became aware of their true identity, and began receiving Messages from them on a regular basis. Prior to 2003, she was a well-known operatic soprano under her professional name, Marilyn Zschau, and sang for over thirty-five years all over the globe on five of the seven continents.

She is also a Certified Clinical Hypnotherapist specializing in Past Life Regression Therapy as well as a trained Reiki Practitioner and Holder of the Usui-Hayashi-Takata-Fran Brown-Mary Goslen-Marilyn Zschau Baars Lineage of Usui

Satori Reiki. She and her husband, Franciscus Joseph Baars, have founded and are Co-Directors of Archangel Healing, and have the distinct pleasure of transmitting the healing energies and messages of The Archangels directly to clients.

Marilyn and her husband Frans live in Oakland, California with their two cats and enjoy outings to Mt. Shasta, San Francisco, and Monterey, as well as walks in the wooded hills behind their home. They have an office in downtown Oakland for Archangel Healing sessions, and welcome all who desire to connect to The Archangels to contact them.

Email Address: archangelhealing@gmail.com

Website Address: www.archangel-healing.com